WHERE THE SOUTHERN CROSS
THE YELLOW DOG

Carroll Cloar, *Where the Southern Cross the Yellow Dog*, Memphis Brooks Museum of Art, © The Estate of Carroll Cloar.

WHERE THE SOUTHERN CROSS
THE YELLOW DOG

On Writers and Writing

LOUIS D. RUBIN, JR.

University of Missouri Press   Columbia and London

Copyright © 2005 by
The Curators of the University of Missouri
University of Missouri Press, Columbia, Missouri 65201
Printed and bound in the United States of America
All rights reserved
5 4 3 2 1   09 08 07 06 05

Library of Congress Cataloging-in-Publication Data

Rubin, Louis Decimus, 1923-
    Where the Southern cross the Yellow Dog : on writers and
writing / Louis D. Rubin, Jr.
        p.   cm.
    Includes index.
    Summary: "Examines the problems facing the American
literary scene, including creative writing programs, sports
writing, Southern literature, publishing, and poetry, with
references to William Faulkner, Eudora Welty, James Joyce,
Thomas Wolfe, Mark Twain, Joyce Carol Oates, T. S. Eliot,
William Wordsworth, Samuel Taylor Coleridge, Herman
Melville, and Ernest Hemingway"—Provided by publisher.
    ISBN-13: 978-0-8262-1608-3 (alk. paper)
    ISBN-10: 0-8262-1608-0 (alk. paper)
    1. Authorship.   2. American literature—Southern
States—History and criticism.   3. American literature—
History and criticism.   4. English literature—History
and criticism.   5. Southern States—Intellectual life.
6. Southern States—In literature.   I. Title.
    PS3568.U26W47   2005
    810.9'975—dc22   2005013944

♾ ™ This paper meets the requirements of the
American National Standard for Permanence of Paper
for Printed Library Materials, Z39.48, 1984.

Designer: Kristie Lee
Typesetter: Phoenix Type, Inc.
Printer and binder: Thomson-Shore, Inc.
Typefaces: Adobe Garamond and Copperplate

For four good poets
Rosanne Coggeshall, Jane Gentry,
Elizabeth Seydel Morgan, and Marly Youmans

and two good editors
Mary Flinn and Shannon Ravenel

CONTENTS

PREFACE AND
ACKNOWLEDGMENTS

～⌒

This book is about writing, and about those who write, teach, edit, or otherwise practice writing, whether as craft, sullen art, trade, curriculum, or obsession. I believe I can speak out of some familiarity with all those modes and more.

By the time I was twelve years old, in the mid-1930s, I had become permanently addicted to the odor of printer's ink and paper, and since then there have been few things connected with writing and publishing that I haven't tried. For a while I even kept a press in our basement, from which experience I learned that there is no way to publish a book that is totally free of typos, even if you set the type yourself by hand. Nowadays all is done with computers, but the premise holds.

After the war—which war? *our* war—I set out to be a newspaperman, but instead became a teacher. I have taught some writers, and edited others, who were considerably more gifted than myself. In 1982, together with Shannon Ravenel I started a small trade publishing house, Algonquin Books. For lack of capital to stay the course we ended up having to sell it after a half-dozen years. To put it another way, my editorial talents proved superior to my financial skills. We did manage to launch some excellent young novelists on their careers, which was the main objective.

In doing all the above I have formed some notions about authors, editors, publishers, and readers. The pieces that follow are an attempt to set a few of these down on paper. Some were written specifically for this book, and the others might as well have been, for they grew out of the same set of compulsions and prejudices. To varying degrees, most have been revised for this volume. There is even so a certain amount of repetition, I hope not too much.

Four of these pieces appeared first in the *Sewanee Review,* for which I have been writing a series of commentaries for more than a quarter century, under the general heading of "Encaustics." Of these, "Our Absolutely Deplorable Literary Situation" was included in an earlier book of mine, but has sufficiently to do with this book's theme that I venture to reprint it. In its general tone no doubt it reflects some of my chagrin at having failed to keep Algonquin Books afloat independently. It was written in 1993, but alas, most of what I had to say then about literary publishing apparently still holds good, only more so with the advent of e-mail. In retrospect, however, several of the proposed "remedies" seem even more impractical than they did at the time, while by contrast the Internet seems to be offering a new way to circulate good poetry.

The contents of this book were written as familiar essays, not scholarly treatises. Page citations are included only when I thought the reader might want to explore the full context of what is being quoted. Also, though by far the larger and more gifted part of the students and authors I have worked with as a teacher and editor have been women, I have been unable to come up with a practical substitute for the masculine pronoun to indicate the third-person hypothetical singular. To echo General Lee's Farewell Order, "I need not tell the survivors of so many hard fought battles, who have remained steadfast to the last, that I have consented to this result from no distrust of them."

As noted herein, the novelist Stendhal liked to dedicate his work to what he termed "The Happy Few," meaning the enlightened readers of a less hypocritical future era. I can make no such assumption about anything that I have written. What I prefer to keep in mind is a remark attributed to Louis Armstrong: "There's some people that, if they don't already know, there's no use trying to tell them."

Portions of the following essays were originally published in the *Sewanee Review,* not necessarily under the same titles, and I am grateful to the editor, George Core, and to the University of the South for permission to reprint them. To wit:

"Slugging It Out with Dempsey and Others," 108:3 (Summer 2000): 412–32

"Bloom's Leap: Or, How Firm a Foundation," 101:1 (Winter 1993): 88–97

"The Progress of Poetry: Or, a Funny Thing Happened on the Way to the Bookstore," 103:3 (Winter 1995): 412–32

"Our Absolutely Deplorable Literary Situation—and Some Thoughts on How to Fix It Good," 102:4 (Fall 1994): 612–20

The last was included in Louis D. Rubin, Jr., *Babe Ruth's Ghost and Other Historical and Literary Speculations* (Seattle and London: University of Washington Press, 1996).

An earlier version of parts of "Questions of Intent: Some Thoughts on Author-ship" appeared in *Virginia Quarterly Review* 73 (Spring 1997): 204–24, under the title of "Criticism and Fiction: Observations by a Jack-leg Practitioner." I am grateful to the late Staige Blackford for publishing it, and to Theodore S. Genoways for permission to reprint such of it as is included in this book.

"Thoughts on Fictional Places" appeared first in *Place in American Fiction: Excursions and Explorations,* edited by H. L. Weatherby and George Core (Columbia: University of Missouri Press, 2004), 33–44.

For permission to reproduce the painting *Where the Southern Cross the Yellow Dog,* by Carroll Cloar, © The Estate of Carroll Cloar, I am indebted to Ms. Patricia S. Cloar, of Oxford, Mississippi, and to Ms. Kip Peterson of the Memphis Brooks Museum of Art, Memphis, Tennessee.

WHERE THE SOUTHERN CROSS
THE YELLOW DOG

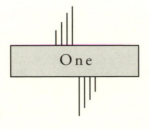

One

THE ORDEAL OF
UNCONSTANT MOOSE

I once knew a barber in Baltimore who wrote poems. Whenever I stopped by his shop he had a new poem for me to read. He liked to describe himself as the Perry Como of poesy, referring to the popular singer who had begun his professional career as a barber.

In the course of his reading he had assembled a supply of literary expressions, but having encountered most of them in books rather than in conversation, he was not always sure about the pronunciations. Once when I came in for my monthly haircut there was no new poem. "I got me an unconstant moose," he explained. I had a momentary vision of a large, shaggy, imposing if flighty ruminant of the northern forests, until I realized that what he had in mind was one of the Sacred Nine, the mythological muses of the arts and sciences, together with the title of Margaret Kennedy's novel *The Constant Nymph,* or perhaps the movie made from it.

Unconstant Moose is an apt characterization of the recurring ailment known also as Writer's Block, or Creative Hang-up, which at one time or the other is known to afflict most authors whose work importantly involves the use of imagination. There it is, massive, hirsute, inchoate, its imposing antlers spread aloft like a gantry crane. Depending upon the individual sufferer and the nature of what is being written, the presence of Unconstant Moose can thwart the process of literary composition for hours, days, and even months at a time. Nor is its incidence restricted to writers of poetry, fiction, or drama alone. History, critical analysis, interpretive

1

journalism, any kind of writing that entails something more rigorous than the nonjudgmental recording of factual data, can expose the author to victimization.

A writer preparing to practice his craft is like a sailor about to embark on an offshore voyage. Once he heads down the channel and reaches deep water there can be no turning back; he will have committed his boat and himself. It is scarcely surprising, therefore, that he may experience a certain internal queasiness and a reluctance to cast off the dock lines. Is the bilge pump working properly? Is there any oil in the bilge? What is tomorrow's weather forecast? Why not run the Waterway instead of going outside? For that matter, why not put off this trip until next week?

For the author about to set forth on a new opus, alternatives to beginning work present themselves, as often as not putting in an appearance just as the writing project is about to get under way. There are a couple of more books on related topics that should be read. The top of the desk must be cleared off and straightened up, and certain letters and documents filed away. Correspondence is uncovered that cannot be permitted to go any longer without reply. The front lawn has absolutely got to be mowed that very day. The family dog must be taken to the vet for a bath and trim. The garage door needs replacement and painting. Do I really wish to begin this particular book at this particular time?

The writer, however, is resolute, determined that Today Is the Day. No more thinking about and talking about writing; it is time for him to get down to the nitty-gritty. Determinedly he takes up position at his desk. He stares at the blank sheet of paper, or at the computer screen. Its opaque emptiness is accusatory; he must *do* something.

At the top center of the page he writes CHAPTER 1. Below it a sentence of text is needed. *For a long time I used to go to bed early.* Somebody has already used that. *Call me Ishmael.* Likewise. Besides, what the hell do I know about whales? Hmm . . . All of a sudden his mind is a blank.

At that point there are a variety of options available to him. The writer may:

- Look out the window and watch a squirrel as it works to extract sunflower seeds from a bird feeder
- Clean and polish his eyeglasses

- De-wax his hearing aid
- If writing in longhand, sharpen some pencils or test the ink flow of a pen. If using a computer, open up a paper clip and remove the lint, dog hair, and crumbs from between the rows of the keyboard. If using a typewriter, replace the ribbon, then go into the bathroom and, using soap and water, scrub the ink off his hands
- Check the calendar to see whether he has a dentist's appointment next week
- Discover an unpaid utilities bill, write a check for it, address and place a stamp on the envelope, and take it out to the mailbox
- If today's mail has arrived, read it
- Remember that he didn't put the trash out
- Put it out
- Go ahead and mow the front lawn
- Do anything else that comes to mind along these lines

No single such response is evidence that trouble is in the offing. On the contrary, each will doubtless appear, to the observer and above all to the writer himself, to be a natural, even reflexive action preparatory to the act of writing—and indeed it might be. Beyond doubt, the act of literary composition involves the marshaling of intellectual and emotional resources; a certain amount of windup is understandable. Did not Caesar pause before crossing the Rubicon? Did not Eisenhower check the weather report before proceeding with D-day?

Let us, therefore, not leap to conclusions. Not until one such symptom manifests itself and another promptly shows up should suspicion arise. The warning alert blinks amber. Let a third symptom appear, not necessarily in the sequence listed above, and the possibility can no longer be ignored. The amber has changed to red. What had seemed at first to be no more than momentary wariness, a fleeting oscillation of attention, may be the Real Decoy: i.e., Unconstant Moose.

Although by no means restricted to the opening moments of the act of writing, the behavior I have described is characteristic of such occasions. The chances are that if Unconstant Moose is about to strike, it will reveal itself either at the start or fairly early along the way. The reason for this should be obvious. Whatever preparations the author may have previously undertaken in the way of notes, documentation, outlines, scenarios, diagrams, plotting, maps, even the jotting down of possible images, ideas, and snatches of dialogue, the fact remains that an actual writing commitment still remains to be made. It has been a matter of conjecture, an assertion of honorable intentions. Even if, say, a book contract has been signed and an advance in royalties accepted and spent, psychologically the writing project remains something that is scheduled to take place at a future time. To echo Emily Dickinson, "I dwell in Possibility—a fairer house than prose."

With the application of words onto paper or computer screen, however, all that will change. A work-in-progress will then exist—an entity in its own right, palpable, incomplete, requiring further development. *Alea jacta est:* jacks or better to open. The die is cast. *Rien ne va plus.* At so crucial a moment, is it any wonder that the writer might be tempted to back away from the brink?

The effort to evade this opening authorial moment of truth can assume varied and sometimes bizarre forms, depending upon the individual author and the nature of what is being avoided. Persons who mean to begin books have been known to sell their automobiles and household goods and move to Italy or France, on the assumption that some locales are more "stimulating" than others. Certainly it is plausible that one is more likely to find himself in a creative mood in an apartment overlooking the Piazza di Spagna or the Champs Elysée instead of across from a block of row houses in North Philadelphia, Pennsylvania.

The exact opposite, however, can also be argued: that the fewer the distractions, scenic or otherwise, the better the ability to concentrate. The novelist Alex Haley, a Coast Guard veteran, used to make extended voyages aboard passenger-carrying freighters in order to write, the theory being, I suppose, that the view from a porthole in the middle of the ocean was less likely to draw his attention away from the typewriter. Provided the weather is decent, this is plausible.

What it comes down to is that there are people who can write anywhere, under any conditions short of total uproar, and other people who find it necessary to settle into a habitual routine amid familiar surroundings before the words will begin to flow.

Back in the mid-1930s the *Saturday Evening Post* carried a full-page advertisement showing the novelist Booth Tarkington, pencil in hand, at work on a manuscript, together with a testimonial from him to the effect that Dixon Ticonderoga pencils were essential to his writing. Doubtless this explained to numerous less prolific authors why they had been unable to get going on their books; they had been attempting to write with Eberhard Fabers. I knew a newspaper columnist who fully intended to write a novel, but the typewriter he used at home was old and cumbersome, so before he could settle into the job he would first have to purchase a better machine. As far as I know he never did.

Nowadays the development of computers has notably facilitated the physical chore of writing. Because what has been written can be changed or canceled so easily before being printed, the stark finality of inscribing words upon paper has been mitigated. Yet the blessing is not unmixed, because the very ease of making revisions encourages the author to keep fiddling around with what has already been written, instead of getting on with the job.

Another possible manifestation of Unconstant Moose is the sudden development of a need to write something other than what one has sat down to write. Almost anything—book reviews, essays, poems, short stories, even a different book—will do. As Marcel Proust wrote about just such matters, "how many tasks are undertaken in order to avoid that one!" (I have found that editing the writings of others is very useful in this respect.)

Proust described the creation of a work of art, literary or otherwise, as "the most real of all things, the sternest school in life and truly the Last Judgment." What I believe he had in mind was the obligation to make use of one's talents—which after a tardy start Proust certainly did manage to do. All the same, to depict the ability to wrestle successfully with Unconstant Moose as emblematic of moral worthiness would appear to place a grievous burden upon the metabolisms of authors. Theologically at least, it ought to be possible to be allowed into Heaven without having to write a book.

Devotee though I am of Proust, I think that, for reasons having ultimately to do with autobiography more than aesthetics, he placed too great an emphasis on artistic creativity as a redemptive act. Is it always true, as he insists, that "instinct dictates the duty to be done and intelligence supplies the excuses for evading it"? In terms of making use of one's literary gifts, might it not sometimes work the other way around? An author might realize quite well what he ought to be writing, but instinctively wish to write something else.

Like preaching, writing has been described as a profession to which many are called but few are chosen. If so, it may well be that Unconstant Moose has a role to play in the selection process. Anyone who has worked for a publishing house is familiar with the avalanche of book-length manuscripts that arrive daily in the mail. Almost all have been written by authors who are convinced that a literary career beckons. Most are unpublishable and beyond salvaging. One is reminded of the hoary story of the Tennessee farm youth who showed up at the admissions office of the theological seminary at Vanderbilt University. He had been out in the field plowing, he said, and had seen a vision. The clouds overhead had been shaped into the letters "P C," instructing him to Preach Christ. He had at once put away the horse and plow, and departed the farm for the seminary. After chatting with the youth for a while, the admissions officer assured him that undeniably his vision had been real, but that he had misinterpreted the message. What the letters "P C" stood for was Plant Corn. Ouch.

It is possible that a writer may be endowed with so abundant a supply of high resolve that he will be immune to the customary authorial alibis, excuses, and subterfuges. To launch him along his carefully marked course he has worked out a set of procedures, involving outlines, notes, etc., so that, having begun to write, almost before he knows it he finds himself several dozen manuscript pages into his intended book. Damn the torpedoes, full speed ahead! He is over the hump.

As indeed he may be. Let him not relax his vigilance just yet, however. For at some point, say midway into his second chapter, he may discover himself faltering, the words coming harder, the sentences tailing off. Soon he may pause in midparagraph. Does what I am writing mean what I intend for it to mean? Is my argument convincing? Do I believe it myself?

He decides to examine what has been written so far, in order to spot where he may have begun to drift off course. It is a Known Fact that there are times when what has been written will appear to the author to better or to worse advantage than at other times. He turns back to Chapter 1, page 1, begins to read—and is appalled. What had seemed so plausible, so masterfully told, so, well, *inevitable,* now looks lifeless and contrived. And where it is *headed?* The thesis appears cut-and-dried; the narrative trail has grown cold. In short, having cleverly disguised itself to resemble its very antithesis, Unconstant Moose has struck again. There may be good writers whose record of performance indicates that they were or are immune to this uncertainty, but I doubt it. Not even Anthony Trollope.

Do not get the notion that so-called creative writers—novelists, poets, dramatists—are the only writers who can be victimized by Unconstant Moose. The author of Ecclesiastes was obviously well acquainted with the problem. Good historians can be prime targets. Here, for example, is Winston Churchill, of all people, writing to his wife in 1925. At age fifty he has just completed two volumes of *The World Crisis,* his history of the Great War: "I have decided not to try the third volume and to retire from the literary arena, at any rate for some time to come."

Imaginative writing is a mode of thinking, requiring the continuous expenditure of both intellect and emotion. Practicing it can provide immense satisfaction, which is the principal though by no means the only reason anyone does it. But—it can require hard work. The natural tendency is to postpone or delay the latter for as long as possible.

Being on the whole a fairly sophisticated lot, good writers are aware of the temptation on their part to do just that. Yet the open, uncomplicated acceptance of the urge to knock off work will never do. Perish forbid! Instead it is necessary to apply sleight of hand. I have suggested a few of what is almost an infinite number of such possible responses: the writer assures himself that his pencils need sharpening, that he had better make sure of a reference, that the trash has not been taken outside, and so on. And indeed lead pencils do require sharpening; references must be accurately used; trash does have to be taken out. Even so, the sudden discovery, prior to or during the act of literary composition, of an urgent need to perform such tasks is no more a matter of mere coincidence than is the appearance of costumed ghouls and goblins on All Hallows Eve or of maidens weaving ribbons around maypoles when the sap rises in the springtime.

Writers caught in the grip of Unconstant Moose have also been known to attribute the difficulties they are encountering in their work to other and graver causes. When reading prose or poetry in which the burden of the authorial argument is a lamentation over the failure to perform professionally, it is usually a good idea to question whether Unconstant Moose, rather than what the writer is claiming, might be the culprit, no matter how plausible the latter may sound. Thus, is John Milton's sonnet entitled "On His Blindness" (the poet himself did not give it that title) really about eye trouble?

> When I consider how my light is spent
> Ere half my days in this dark world and wide,
> And that one talent which 'tis death to hide
> Lodged in me useless . . .

And what of Samuel Johnson's claim that "no one but a blockhead ever wrote but for money"? Was the celebrated "person from Porlock" who interrupted Coleridge while at work the true reason that "Kubla Khan" was left unfinished? (If only an outbreak of Unconstant Moose had smitten Tennyson about halfway through "Maud.") Writers can be deceptive fellows. I am even a little suspicious of T. S. Eliot when he had J. Alfred Prufrock remark, "It is impossible to say just what I mean!"

It must be emphasized that in the majority of cases of Unconstant Moose (I almost wrote Unconscious Moose) considerably more than conscious deception is involved. If that were all there was to it, then a little willpower alone would be sufficient to send it packing. At least as important to its advent, however, is the role of memory, which is to say, the relationship, whether direct or implicit, of what is being written about to the writer's previous experience, and the associations that are thereby touched off. If to write is to think on paper, and if literary creativity has to do with authorial emotion as well as authorial cogitation, then no inconsiderable portion of the problem can be a reluctance to revisit, however obliquely, unpleasant aspects of the writer's experience.

It goes almost without saying that there are countering forces at work, or otherwise very little would ever get written. For one thing, there is the very nature of literary creativity itself. The writer *wants* to tell a story, write a poem, develop an essay. More than that, he is *drawn* to his subject matter. There is the urge to make sense of it. Very few writers were drafted into their vocation; on the contrary, the compulsion to write comes from within. The need to confront volatile personal material can be the source of tremendous strength. As such it can attract writers, and also cause them to shy away—not infrequently at one and the same time. There is the wish to exhibit, and the wish to hide. In the tension between these two impulses lies much of what makes for good imaginative writing.

Most writers rather enjoy holding forth on the vicissitudes and rigors of their craft. An entire anthology could be compiled of what writers have had to say on their creative problems. (Compiling it, of course, might be yet another way of avoiding the writing of a book.) It should be kept in mind that literary composition is at bottom a private activity. Even someone like Churchill, who once he could afford to do so employed young historians as research associates and even had them produce draft passages of text, must ultimately toil alone with language and make the choices for himself. This basic professional isolation being what it is, the urge to tell others about how difficult the creative vigil can be (*vide* the present opus) should not be surprising.

This is not to say that a writer is without justification for so wishing. An understandable grievance of just about every good author is that persons who haven't themselves made a serious attempt to write are convinced that it is an easy way to earn a living. A common assumption is that the act of writing consists of no more than a direct one-for-one jotting down of one's thoughts. Anyone who wishes to write, the notion goes, can do it. That language is other than a transparent casing for objects and ideas, and that something beyond routine diligence is needed to use it well, seldom occurs to most people. There is the story of the elder Dumas being confronted by an acquaintance who announced that he had discovered his secret: you hire other writers to write your chapters, the critic declared, and all you do is to splice together what they write. "Ah, my friend, you have found me out," Dumas replied. "Now let's see you do it!"

The novelist Thomas Wolfe liked to tell about his mother, who upon learning that he had been paid $1,500 by the *Saturday Evening Post* for a short story remarked admiringly that he was the first member of the family who was able to earn that much money without having to work hard for it. On this particular complaint even Wolfe's most vehement antagonist, the novelist-critic Bernard DeVoto, was in agreement with him. DeVoto, who had unpleasant things to say about Wolfe's unabashed self-absorption and rhetorical excess, cited another novelist's remark about an inability to make his wife understand "that if I'm staring out of the window I'm working." At such times, DeVoto insisted in *The World of Fiction* (1950), the novelist "is working—harder, probably, than when he is at his desk. He is working most of the time. During his most intensely busy moments he is likely to seem to an outsider a loafer wasting time as pointlessly as the crowd that watches a steam-shovel excavating a basement."

Perhaps the most eloquent assertion of the Case of the Inadequately Appreciated Author was set forth by the poet Yeats:

> Better go down upon your marrow-bones
> And scrub a kitchen pavement, or break stones
> Like an old pauper, in all kinds of weather;
> For to articulate sweet sounds together
> Is to work harder than all these, and yet
> Be thought an idler...
>
> ("Adam's Curse")

In any case, and whether justified or not, the advent of Unconstant Moose is a method of protest against the imminent expenditure of the literary equivalent of blood, toil, tears, and sweat. Turn away while you still can, the writer's reflexes are urging him. No, his conscience argues, don't give in. Preach! Write! Act! Once more into the breach, dear comrades!

Caught in this tug-of-war, the writer may decide to stop work for a few days and allow his imagination to percolate on its own; or he may decide to keep grinding out lines and sentences according to plan, in the hope that he can slog his way through the alligators, regain firm footing, and return only later to clean up the swamp.

The obvious American exemplars of these two modes of authorial response are Mark Twain and Henry James. Sam Clemens's approach was to write only for as long as he found the flow of words coming freely.

When he ran into trouble he would put that manuscript aside and go on to something else. James, by contrast, began with an idea, entered it in his notebooks, speculated about it, tried out situations, eventually developed an outline, then produced a detailed scenario, and from that began writing his novel. James produced a shelfload of good fiction as well as some notable nonfiction. Clemens left us several classics of world literature and an vast agglomeration of prose ranging from fair to indifferent fiction, nonfiction, and journalism, much of it abandoned in midpassage. Unconstant Moose, thy name is Samuel L. Clemens!

Yet what James called his Blest Old Genius was no easy taskmaster, either. Here is the conclusion of his American journals, written in 1882 at age thirty-nine:

> If only I can *concentrate* myself: this is the great lesson of life. I have hours of unspeakable reaction against my smallness of production; my wretched habits of work—or of un-work; my levity; my vagueness of mind; my perpetual failure to focus my attention, to absorb myself, to look things in the face, to invent, to produce, in a word.

Methinks the author doth protest too much.

In their efforts to repel the onslaught of Unconstant Moose, most writers are ranged somewhere between the strategies of these two great literary artists. Either they attempt to postpone the confrontation, on the assumption that tomorrow will be better (*Huckleberry Finn* was written in three separate installments), or else they try to work out all the details before they begin to write, so that there will be nothing problematic to hold them up. As for which approach works better, that depends upon the temperament of the writer thus assailed.

Certain general observations of a quasi-metaphysical nature seem appropriate here. It must be remembered that a degree of emotional dissatisfaction with the cosmos and one's place within it is endemic to all authors. If they were fully satisfied with life as they perceive it to be, and with their relationship to it, there would be no need to write, whether in complaint or in affirmation. As it is, either they want the world around them rearranged to fit their own requirements, or else they want it to stay in place permanently and not to change; typically they prefer both. Therefore they experience frustration, and are unhappy.

However, if in that sense all writers are neurotics, by no means are all neurotics writers. (This is known as Rubin's Law.) The difference is that writers, like other creative folk, possess the ability to make use of such emotions, through reshaping them symbolically. They do it with words, in the form of poems, stories, narratives, essays. This does not mean that the elements of conflict thereupon disappear from the writer's life, but rather that these can be identified and understood for what they are, so that they will no longer hinder the ability to function effectively, whether as writer or as citizen. As the poet Wordsworth once announced, "To me alone there came a thought of grief. / A timely utterance gave that thought relief / And I again am strong." Well, maybe…

Where Freud and other early practitioners of psychoanalysis erred was in seeking to explain literary creativity as if an author's writings were no more than wish-fulfilling daydreams, and as if literary talent consisted of a greater-than-ordinary vulnerability to private fantasies. What they did not take into account is the writer's ability to *control* and *apply* his emotional experience, to use it rather than be used by it, which is precisely what the garden-variety neurotic cannot do. Literary artistry is from this standpoint not a compensatory device for coping with maladjustment but a manifestation of strength, a product of the possession and active employment of self-knowledge. It is interesting that Henry James on his deathbed thought that he was Napoleon Bonaparte.

If we think of literary creativity in this way, it follows that the presence of Writer's Block, or Unconstant Moose, is evidence of the existence of creative struggle. Its principal cause, it seems to me, is not so much irresolution or inertia as the author's as-yet-unvoiced suspicion that he does not adequately understand what he proposes to write about, and that he will have to work—work *hard*—to master it. His immediate response may be to try something easier for now, either a less demanding writing project or something not involving writing at all, such as mowing the lawn or watching the Chicago Cubs on television. Or else, as noted earlier, he resolves to keep going, in the belief that by forcing himself to work through it he will eventually figure it out. (The quota system—so many paragraphs or pages, no matter how bad, written daily—is one way to apply the latter strategy.)

Whatever method is used, the fact seems to be that more often than not stories, poems, essays, and books that matter *do* ultimately get written. The "mute, inglorious Milton" theory of potential masterworks thwarted by adverse circumstances is, finally, both unprovable and irrelevant; as readers our concern is with what can be read. The literary project may take months or years to complete. It may turn out to be about something very different from what the author had intended to write. It may have a quite different resolution than originally planned, may even multiply itself into several different works. But either it is written or it is nothing. Whether the would-be author sets it aside for good and takes up gunrunning, or whether he is run over by a Mack truck, cannot figure in our literary experience.

Unconstant Moose, then, is to literary creativity as a call at a yacht-broker's yard in January is to boat ownership, or a visit to a family physician approximately one month after a glorious weekend at a ski lodge is to true love—an indication that there has been imaginative involvement. Nothing may ultimately come of it, and even if it does, considerable confusion may well lie ahead. But the creative potentiality is there, for Writer's Block can function only if there is something to be blocked.

From all that I have seen of the practitioners of what Dylan Thomas termed his "craft or sullen art" of literary composition, any good writer who claims never to have been afflicted with Unconstant Moose is probably lying through his teeth. Either that, or else he really does believe that the lawn cannot go another day without being mowed—in which instance the evidence indicates a hopeless case.

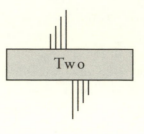

ON THE LITERARY USES
OF MEMORY

We write to make sense of our lives, and some of us can make more sense of it than others. This is a basic function of the literary process. How we do it is one thing; why we feel the need to do it is another. Typically, more than one incentive may be at work.

My concern here is with the kind of imaginative writing whereby the author draws more or less directly on his own earlier experience. In one sense this is what all writers do, since that is the only kind of experience available. What I have in mind, however, are those writings in which people, places, and events drawn from the author's earlier life are made into the specific subject matter of literary works, whether as fiction, poetry, or memoir.

Over and beyond the basic urge to re-create life in language, many things can be active in the communicated personality of a writer. For starters, why did Augustine write his *Confessions?* It was a way of preaching, to be sure: a cautionary text, and as such an accepted theological form. Addressing his words to God throughout his narrative, he prepares to recount, with appropriate commentary, the experience of his youth, his carnal and intellectual wickedness, and his conversion, which was made possible through the grace of God. In so recounting he will not, however, be telling God about anything that God does not already know: "Not to Thee, O my God, but in Thy presence I am telling it to my own kind, to the race of men, or rather to that small part of the human race that may come upon these writings. And to what purpose do I tell it? Simply that I and any other who may read must realize out of what depths we must cry to Thee."*

Wholeheartedly; fervently; but surely not "simply." In addressing his account to God for reading by his fellow humans, the author is making use of a technique of the classical rhetoric he once taught—speaking in order to be overheard. The *Confessions* are not a naive, unsophisticated outpouring, but the shaped product of a master of prose narrative.

In chronicling his earlier misdeeds Augustine was describing his sins. Although elsewhere he insists that one can remember emotional experience without reexperiencing the emotion itself, there must also have been satisfaction taken in chronicling to some detail the process of overcoming his moral weakness and shame. Augustine himself was aware of this dimension: "a man often glories the more vainly for his very contempt of vainglory: for which reason he does not really glory in his contempt of glory: in that he glories in it, he does not condemn it" (book X, no. 38, 205). I am reminded of Winston Churchill's delightful remark to Violet Asquith in 1906: "We are all worms. But I do believe that I am a glow-worm."

As Augustine declares at the outset of the *Confessions,* God would not need to be told that they are written for purposes of religious admonition to others. Perhaps, though, there may be those in his human audience who might be skeptical about his motives in so writing. It may even be that the author wishes to reassure himself. Anyone who reads the *Confessions* must surely be impressed by the psychological insights of this brilliant man. Pride of authorship is not only identified, but dissected.

My point is that Augustine recognized that confessional writing, like all other forms of imaginative literature, has not only a homiletic but also a therapeutic aspect. In composing it, he was confronting the question that lies at the heart of all such writing: Who am I?

Perhaps the most immediate impulse for exploring one's own earlier life is that of nostalgia, the wish to return to an irrecoverable past: irrecoverable *because* it is past. The poet Housman writes of the yearning for "those

* *Confessions,* book II, no. 3, trans. F. J. Sheed (New York: Sheed and Ward, 1942), 24.

blue remembered hills...the land of lost content." Understandably the places and experiences of our earlier years may figure in our memories with a vividness and concreteness that can make our subsequent adult experience seem deficient in staying power. This does not necessarily make such memories enjoyable, but the chances are that, to the degree we willingly seek them out, the "satisfactions of remembrance" are what we are hoping to derive from them.

Obviously there are considerations involved that go beyond—or in any event go together with—nostalgia. We may wish to exorcise from our memories events that were unpleasant and frightening. To restore these to view can be painful, however, and we may prefer to avoid writing about them or else to deal with them only obliquely—yet we can feel compelled to return to them.

There are numerous reasons the human being who is doing the telling may wish to dissemble, whether for purposes of vanity, modesty, self-protection, reluctance to offend or to give pain, sentimentality, or whatever. "Tell the whole Truth, but tell it slant," Emily Dickinson advises in another context. Moreover, the artistic requirements of what is being written have their own agenda and make their own shaping demands.

The novelist Stendhal opens *The Life of Henri Brulard,* a memoir only very lightly camouflaged as fiction, by picturing himself standing on the Janiculum in Rome at age fifty, pondering the question of what it has been all about, and deciding to write the story of his life. By so doing, he says, "then perhaps, at last, when it is finished, I should know what I have been, whether gay or sad, a clever man or a fool, brave or timid; and finally, whether the sum total be happy or unhappy."* When he died in 1842 the manuscript was left unfinished, so no one can say what he may have found out.

What does seem clear is that the process of looking back at his younger days and recording his thoughts about them so intrigued him that repeatedly he set off on tangents, letting his recollections carry him wherever they might go, drawing diagrams of where things were, making heretical political comments, with only sporadic attention to narrative development.

* Trans. Catherine Alison Phillips (New York: A. A. Knopf, 1925), 3.

For the true Beyleist (his full name was Marie Henri Beyle; Stendhal was a pen name) this can make for delightful browsing, but strictly as story-telling it can become vexing.

Whether as novelist, memoirist, or conversationalist, Stendhal had relatively few inhibitions, and whatever his plans for composing *Henri Brulard* may have been, he seems to have felt little or no imperative to tell it slant. On the contrary, he rather enjoyed shocking others with his candor about his past, even at his own expense. He liked to say that he was writing not for contemporaries but for the readers of a future day, "The Happy Few." In the instance of his books, that is exactly what happened.

It is also true that the willingness to rehearse one's misdeeds, weaknesses, and embarrassments in print involves a marked degree of egocentricity. An author who chooses to make himself the subject of his writing volunteers thereby to assume a public stance, and if there is reticence, there is obviously also revelation. What distinguished Stendhal, perhaps, was the zest with which he went about thrusting his personality onto all that he wrote, so that whatever he published was in the nature of a virtuoso performance.

This holds not only for *Henri Brulard* but also for his two finest novels, *The Red and the Black* and *The Charterhouse of Parma,* and his other fiction, as well the numerous memoirs, diaries, manifestos, pronouncements, reviews, travel writings, and correspondence. As French consul at Civitavecchia he could turn a diplomatic report into an exhibition. At the same time his prose style is clear as a bell, without adornment or complication.

This beings us, as almost any discourse on the literature of recall is likely to do, to Marcel Proust. Proust entitled his great multivolume novel *A la recherche de temps perdu*—"In Search of Lost Time."* We might almost

---

* The original English-language edition, entitled *Remembrance of Things Past,* was translated by C. K. Scott-Moncrieff, with the final volume in the American edition by Frederick A. Blossom. There were later translations, based on several-times-revised French texts. The most recent, by various hands working under the overall direction of Christopher Prendergast and given the more accurate title of *In Search of Lost Time,* was published in England by Penguin and is appearing in the United States under the imprint of Viking. At the time of this writing (2004),

think of the novel as Proust's own "Confessions." It is told from the standpoint of one who finally discovers his life's work, and who describes the process that led him to this discovery, beginning in early childhood onward. He did not live to see all of it through publication, but before his death in 1923 it must have been obvious to him that the fame he coveted, the recognition by the public that the onetime seeming dilettante and dabbler in letters was nothing less than a great artist, was assuredly his. What had long appeared to others, including some whose esteem he most valued, and equally to himself as well, as an affair of self-indulgence and largely wasted talents is through diligent recapitulation and artistic reshaping transformed into nothing less than a Vocation. The account not only culminates in that realization but is the vehicle for arriving at it. The literary re-creation of his remembered past functions as a mode of redemption.

The discovery that the narrator makes is not a theological revelation; the narrator of Proust's novel is not a believer in a revealed divinity. To be sure, there is a brief passage midway through, describing the death of the novelist Bergotte, which proposes that the only possible explanation for Bergotte's lifelong dedication to his art can be a reality that exists beyond death, and thus implies the possibility of a Resurrection. But the assertion, which was inserted in the manuscript late in the author's life, is only very tentative, and nowhere else in the vast body of *In Search of Lost Time* is any similar pronouncement to be found.

At the same time, Proust insists that a strictly materialistic interpretation of life is inadequate. Humans are incarcerated in time, and the objects of their striving—love, possession, wealth, fame, power, social distinction—come to nothing. Yet this is not all there is to it. The realization that Marcel—the name he proposes for his protagonist—attains in the closing book of the novel, and that the narrator has been preparing for us from the opening pages onward, is that through subjective memory it is possible to break out from the linear confines of chronology.

The experiences of the senses, as their impact is preserved by memory, and not the deductions made by the rational intellect as such, provide the

---

Swann's Way and *In the Shadow of Young Girls in Flower* have been published. For purposes of consistency I shall be quoting from those two volumes, and for volumes 3 through 7 from the English Penguin Classics paperback edition (2003).

means of escape. If a subjective, sensory event in the past can be recaptured, by dint of being reinvoked by a similar experience in the present, two separate moments in time are joined. The individual consciousness is thereby liberated from chronology and, however briefly, can exist free of its limitations.

What Marcel comes to realize is that as a writer it will be his task to focus all his powers of imagination on the implications of what those memories turn up, combining, extending, exploring, seeking what is general within those particular occasions, so that they can be re-created in language and made independent of time and change. It is in works of art, whether of the literary craftsman, painter, the musician, the sculptor, the architect, or whatever, that what is otherwise imprisoned in transience can achieve an existence beyond lineal time, and its artist-maker, through the joy of re-creating it from within his subjective memory and observation, can share in that reshaping:

> And I understood that all these materials for a literary work were actually my past life, I understood that they had come to me, in frivolous pleasures, in idleness, in tenderness, in sorrow, and that they had been stored up by me without my divining their ultimate purpose, even their survival, any more than a seed does when it lays up a reserve of all the nutrients which will feed the plant. (*Finding Time Again,* trans. Ian Patterson, 207–8)

Yet it is possible, I think, to make too much of the role of involuntary, sensory memory as the "method" of Proust's great novel. The novel's *literary form* is that of the past recaptured, as remembered and explored by a narrator who tells of how he came at last to understand how to go about the work of writing it. That does not, however, necessarily mean that the novel we are reading was actually composed in just that way, or that the realization of how to write it must have taken place as described—as a series of bursts of illumination occurring when an aging, disillusioned Marcel attends a reception at which various of his acquaintances from years back are reencountered.

In actuality the multivolume narrative was written over a period of more than fifteen years, during which much of what happens, including some of the most celebrated episodes, was interpolated and developed within a manuscript that was undergoing continuous revision and reshaping. Not only did Proust's compulsion to rework everything that he wrote necessitate multiple galley proofs and staggering charges for author's corrections, but the six-year gap—1913–1919—between publication of the first two volumes, resulting from the outbreak of the Great War, resulted in a momentous overhauling and enlargement.*

For all that earlier biographers, memoirists, and readers, among them the author's friends and contemporaries, were quick to identify the "originals" of Proust's dazzling gallery of personages, it has since become clear that he drew upon a wide variety of traits, mannerisms, attitudes, interests, and physical features to constitute his characters. As Jean-Yves Tadié remarks in his biography, "The same model provided several characters; a single character stemmed from several models; taking up a line, a page, or an entire episode" (680). Nor was Proust in any way reluctant to rearrange his characters, situations, and events chronologically or geographically, in order to fit his design. In short, *In Search of Lost Time* is a work of literary art, consummately so, and the principles that the author followed in writing it are those of artistic creation.

Proust himself bears some responsibility for the tendency to identify and label the "real-life" models for his people too readily and literally. At one point, for example, his narrator declares that "the essential book, the only true book, was not something the writer needs to invent, in the usual sense of the word, so much as to translate, because it already exists within each of us. The writer's task and duty are those of a translator" (*Finding Time Again,* 199). By "translator" he obviously means one who can interpret imaginatively as well as transliterate accurately; an act of creative judgment is involved.

There is a passage in volume 5, *The Captive,* in which the narrator remarks, as an aside addressed to an unnamed "original" designated as "dear Charles Swann," that "it is already because someone whom you must have considered a little idiot has made you the hero of one of his novels that people are beginning to talk about you again, and perhaps your name

* The reader who is curious about the development of the work in progress will find an extensive account of the process of accretion in Jean-Yves Tadié, *Marcel Proust: A Life,* trans. Euan Cameron (New York: Viking, 2000).

will live on." He cites a painting in the balcony of a Paris club, "where you are standing with Gallifet, Edmond de Polignac and Saint-Maurice." If "people talk so much about the Tissot painting, it is because they can see that there is something of you in the character of Swann" (*The Captive*, trans. Carol Clark, 182).

Charles Swann is a fictional character; the man who appears in the painting together with the other "real-life" Parisians is Charles Haas. (In the first English translation of the novel, C. K. Scott-Moncrieff makes the passage read "my dear Charles ————," leaving the surname blank.) In any event, while what happens in Proust's novel in its details and its cast of characters is drawn from the novelist's life, the *Search* is very much a shaped work, and the shaping involves narrative techniques such as foreshadowing, dramatization, juxtaposition, repetition, intensification, authorial commentary, parallelism, simile, metaphor, literary and political allusion, circumlocution, irony, satire, pastiche, and numerous other devices of rhetoric. Far from being dependent upon the chance discoveries of involuntary memory for either its design or its images, Proust's great multivolume work is the product of a conscious, focused literary artistry, with its enormous range of material assimilated within a unifying, luminous style.

In creating a literary work in which Proust's own experience is being re-created into a narrative that culminates in the belated discovery of a "vocation," much use is made of the protagonist's pitfalls, mishaps, and seeming errors along the way. Moreover, while biographers may look for, and discover, models for Proust's characters, certainly many of their attributes, including both virtues and vices, are drawn from his own self-perception.

"Tell the whole Truth, but tell it slant"; Proust does just that. The author himself was a confirmed homosexual, but the narrator-protagonist of the novel is not. At one point he writes as follows: "A writer should not take offense when inverts give his heroines masculine faces. This mildly deviant behavior is the only means by which the invert can proceed to give full general significance to what he is reading" (*Finding Time Again*, 219). This is precisely the reverse of what Proust does! The most striking examples of the technique are the women in Marcel's life, with their masculine-sounding names: Gilberte, Andrée, Albertine. The extensive dissection of sexual desire and jealousy, so painful to read at times (and sometimes, I think, all too tediously drawn out), has been "translated," as it were, from Proust's own experiences. There are known models, and one in particular, for Proust's great tragicomic homosexual figure the Baron de Charlus, surely among the most memorable characters in all of modern literature, but the ultimate authority for the Baron's thought and actions comes from within.

In writing about homosexual love when he did, Proust was dealing with highly controversial subject matter. It had been done before, but not with anything like the same directness and authenticity. Proust dealt with it as a vice, and more often than not portrayed its practitioners as grotesques, by turns pathetic or comic. He sees it as by its very nature a form of bondage, condemned to frustration and inevitably the cause of loss and suffering.

Throughout the novel, suffering is pronounced as essential to artistic insight. "Let [the writer's] intelligence begin the work, plenty of sorrows will arise along the way and look after the business of finishing it. As for happiness, almost its only useful quality is to make unhappiness possible" (*Finding Time Again,* 216). It is true that, for Proust, all human love, whether homosexual or heterosexual, is doomed to disappointment and failure, taking place as it does within chronological time and based on the assumption that inevitably it is an unequal relationship, in that there is one who loves and one who allows himself or herself to be loved. It is also true that none of the three great artist figures in the novel, the novelist Bergotte, the composer Vinteuil, and the painter Elstir, is depicted as homosexual. Yet the equation *homosexuality = suffering = art* seems to me to be fundamental to Proust's view of the elements in his own life that led him toward the writing of his novel.

In his eloquent discourse in volume 4, *Sodom and Gomorrah,* on the misfortunes that homosexuals must endure, he describes them as "sons without a mother, to whom they are obliged to lie even in the hour when they close her eyes" (trans. John Sturrock, 19). It was not a coincidence that the decision to write his novel grew out of a manuscript he was working on in 1908, following his mother's death three years before.

"Contre Sainte-Beuve" began as an essay and developed into an imagined dialogue with his mother, on the subject of whether biographical knowledge of an author should be a major factor in the interpretation of his art. Marcel argues that it should not be; the work of art, he insists, is the product of "a different self from the self we manifest in our habits, in our social life, in our vices."* It was not long before the dialogue underwent the metamorphosis into what became the *Search*.

Certainly Proust, who was passionately attached to his mother and devastated by her death, felt guilt, not only for his sexual preferences but also for his apparent indolence, his failure to pursue a career, his snobbery and fondness for the company of aristocracy, his financial extravagance, his too-willing acquiescence in ill-health, his impracticality. At the same time, inevitably there had been resentment and occasional outright rage over his emotional and financial dependence on her, the need to dissemble his homosexuality, and her persistent efforts to make him lead a more "normal" life. In William C. Carter's words, "if he had been unable to break free, she, too, had been incapable of controlling the great maternal affection that so often spoiled and indulged him" (401).

There is a famous scene, early in *Swann's Way*, in which the family entertains Charles Swann, who lives nearby in Combray, at dinner, and the child Marcel is sent up to bed without his mother's good-night kiss. Unable and unwilling to go to sleep, he defies the rules by waiting on the staircase, until at last the dinner ends and Swann departs. When the child's parents come up to bed, they find him there. The mother's immediate response is anger at his disobedience, but the father, observing the child's unhappiness, tells her to go off to bed with him and comfort him.

The remembering narrator's interpretation of the incident, which he considers to be crucial to his subsequent difficulties, is revealing. For the enduring emotional consequences he blames not his mother but his father. His mother, he insists, had recognized that her son must learn the self-discipline needed to resist giving in to his impulses, while his father was not sufficiently concerned for his son's ultimate well-being to be stern with him. "And so, for the first time, my sadness was regarded no longer as a punishable offense but as an involuntary ailment that had just been officially recognized, a nervous condition for which I was not responsible; I had the relief of no longer having to mingle qualms of conscience with

* Quoted in William C. Carter, *Marcel Proust: A Life* (New Haven: Yale University Press, 2000), 466.

the bitterness of my tears, I could cry without sin" (*Swann's Way*, trans. Lydia Davis, 38).

In other words, his father, by permitting him to be comforted by his mother when unhappy, is therefore responsible for the adult Marcel's moral failings! All in all, a rather strained bit of reasoning. Moreover, the insights of a clinical psychiatrist are not required for the reader to perceive that the child has in effect outmaneuvered his father for his mother's company and good-night kiss.

I noted that there was a "confessional" aspect to *In Search of Lost Time*. That is, the author exerts himself to divulge, at length and in detail, those errors, weaknesses, and turpitudes of which he has been guilty. These are presented either more or less openly, as in his possessiveness, excessive dependence, voyeurism, and taste for social climbing, or else indirectly and obliquely, as with the homosexuality. (As Carter points out, while the protagonist has no homosexual tendencies, he is "suspiciously well-informed and fascinated by the subject" [870, n. 55].)

At the same time there is an element of self-vindication, which manifests itself most conclusively in the narrator's discovery, in the culminating episode of the novel, that his seemingly purposeless and frivolous life has in reality constituted an artistic vocation. Without realizing it, he has been preparing himself all along to *write about it*—to re-create and interpret what he has learned, through involvement, suffering, observation, and reflection, of human love, desire, jealousy, art and artifice, dilettantism, aristocracy, snobbery and social climbing, sadism, self-indulgence, venality, heroism, homosexuality, lesbianism. Now he will write the book—a book that, inasmuch as we have just read it, attests to the validity of the claim. As well it might!

Art thus redeems the human being who is otherwise trapped in time and loss, through enabling him to create a reality which is independent of chronology and superior to loss and sorrow. So that the day when the narrator's task becomes clear to him is "this most glorious day" which "illuminated suddenly not only the old fumblings of my thought, but even the purpose of my life and perhaps of art" (*Finding Time Again*, 195).

The ultimate explanation for Proust's literary art, the one indispensable stimulus, is his passionate, unflagging desire to construct a simulacrum of life in language as such, which is to say, to *write*. In suggesting a few of the motivating impulses that may have figured in Proust's great novel, I hope I have not conveyed the impression that I think they can account for his genius. The elements I have noted can help to determine the form that a literary work may take; they may serve to direct and focus the author's interests; but what distinguishes the genuine artist from either the dilettante or the hack is not the origins of his motivation but the sustaining intensity of his creative vision.

To lower the tone of this critical discourse decisively, let me say that on several occasions I have had a go at so-called autobiographical fiction myself, to no notable result. What I did learn from the attempt is that one cannot compel such fiction to conform to actual remembered events, emotions, or people. Setting aside the question of why we might feel any obligation to do that in the first place, there is the plain fact that storytelling develops its own logic and enforces its own notions of causality. When we try to make a situation develop in a certain way because that is what "really" happened, the characters may begin acting up, so that what takes place in our narrative will not signify what we had in mind, but instead become something else entirely, even something quite contradictory. We may persist in trying to impose compliance with our intentions, only to find that the more we insist—and we can go on insisting for long pages at a time—the less convincing the result may be.

For all the magnificent fusion of detail and meaning in Proust, for example, there are times when the author seems to be attempting to force the evidence to bear out his thesis. The young aristocrat Robert de Saint-Loup may in his middle years turn out to be a homosexual, as the narrator informs us, but based upon the lineaments of his characterization as developed up until then, it is not very believable. Nor do I really believe that the Prince de Guermantes would ever have ended up marrying Mme. Verdurin, for all that it may bear out the author's demonstration of the transience of seemingly permanent social divisions.

Had these things taken place in the course of a straight historical memoir, we might find them astounding but, subject of course to the reliability of the source, would not think to question whether they could plausibly have happened. For a work of fiction, however, they had better be consistent with the characterizations, or else we withhold our assent. The narrative voice, in Proust's book the "I," to that extent loses its credibility, and instead we see not the authorial voice, which is in essence a formal, literary creation, but the biographical Marcel Proust at work manipulating his evidence.

To the extent that we seek to shape our past experience into fiction, our emotions can often be a more reliable guide to the meaning of what happened than our strict adherence to factual memories, because in exploring our feelings we are apt to draw upon resources that run deeper than our immediate, conscious assumptions. Sensory images, not abstract ideas, are what trigger our emotional response, just as Proust says, and through allowing our imagination to follow where our emotions lead, we begin to identify patterns, connections, relationships between what had been seemingly disconnected events.

Thus someone seeking to write about remembered experience can sometimes make more sense of it through allowing himself to fill in gaps in his memory and to build bridges between separate recollected events with imagined developments, conjectures, and random details, and by combining material from more than one memory. (This is one reason it is risky to identify fictional characters too specifically and definitely with their supposed "real-life" counterparts.) Something can be made more faithful to the meaning of an experience through being translated into a different configuration. This is the method of art.

We have to ask ourselves, then, not whether what we are setting down in words is an exact, literal reproduction of the way it "really" happened, but whether it is an honest account of the meanings that are implicit within a remembered event. Authenticity is the ultimate artistic criterion; but that is not identical with photographic realism.

Such are the perils, or a few of them, that can confront the author who sets out to write what the librarian in Joyce's *Ulysses* refers to as "the book of myself." As for the benefits that can result, these include not only the satisfactions that attend the creation of any work of art, literary or otherwise, but also the knowledge that can come from recognizing and identifying, if only imperfectly, the continuity inherent in one's own self. From the multiformity and seeming randomness of our experience, the trail of impressions, events, ideas, and emotions that stretches back almost to our beginnings, through the process of re-creation we may begin to discern some of the patterns and urgencies that have given direction and shape to our lives. In the long run, I believe, it is this last that matters most.

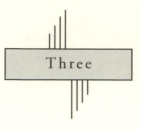

WHERE THE SOUTHERN CROSS
THE YELLOW DOG: A TIME,
A PLACE, A PAINTING

A railroad grade crossing. A set of tracks leads vertically upward, the space between the steel rails narrowing as they ascend; another, partly obscured by underbrush, stretches horizontally across. Together they form the shape of an A, although at the point where the vertical tracks seem to join at the horizon they pass out of sight without actually touching, while the horizontal tracks extend out to both edges of the painting, so that the design is more like that of an artist's easel. At left, above, taking up one-fourth of the surface of the painting, is a tree in full fall foliage. There are more trees along the vertical right-of-way on both sides, leading to the horizon. On the left is a paved road, and along the right, less visible, another. At middle distance on the right is a building, and above it, only lightly in sight and seemingly floating in the sky, is a water tank.

A siding curves off to the left from the tracks, with a white signal disk atop the nearby switch. A red boxcar is in place, too far away for its wheels to be seen. Telegraph poles, at uneven height, are spaced along the right-hand side of the picture, reaching above the frieze of trees. The open area along the roadbed and across the lower portion of the painting on both sides of the tracks is matted with brush, weeds, and grass, leached to copper and straw. The leaves on the trees at the left, and on several of those at the right, are orange-red. The only green in sight is in the trees and bushes at

28

the edge of the right-of-way, and that too is turning. Otherwise, except for the remote blue sky and light cirrus clouds, everything is in shades of russet, saffron, and tan.

Along the horizontal trackage, just to the right of the crossing, a black man and woman are walking. The man is in the act of stepping over a vertical rail, and the woman follows close by. She is wearing a vermilion sweater, and the man wears a brown jacket with a high collar.

The horizon where the vertical tracks disappear from sight is at the visual center of the painting. To achieve that effect the scene is depicted as if viewed from a point directly above the vertical tracks, which are farthest apart at the lower edge of the painting and converge as they lead up the line. The viewer's eye at once translates this shape into distance; we are schooled in the use of linear recession on a two-dimensional surface to produce the perspective of depth.

Straight through the intersection without interruption the vertical rails thrust, with no break in the smooth steel ribbons, continuing up to and beyond the horizon. If a train were to attempt to move through the crossing along the horizontal trackage it would be derailed, for there are no gaps in the vertical rails for the wheel flanges to pass through. Moreover, on either side of the vertical tracks at the crossing are boards, extending across the horizontal rails.

The painter's technique, a modified pointillism, is essentially representational and is by no means emotionally neutral. The stippled effect employed for the foliage and the countless tiny brown stalks of sedge and brush serves to produce a kind of haze, across which the rigidity of the trackage bisects the overwhelming stillness of the roadbed and right-of-way, the golds and cinnamons of the leaves and underbrush, and the squared planes of the buildings. The autumn tones suffuse everything, including the clothes and for that matter the couple themselves. The man's orange-and-white baseball cap and the woman's vermilion sweater, far from clashing with the overall mood of the painting, help to enforce it.

Intent upon their own purposes, the two people crossing the tracks interrupt the immobility of the scene only for as long as it will take them to traverse it. Everything else depicted by the artist, whether natural or manmade—the trees, the shrubbery and brush, the mill to the right of the tracks, the line of telegraph poles, the several small white buildings at the edge of the right-of-way—appears stylized, an array of forms and shapes.

A train that came cruising along those tracks would very likely roll right through town without so much as slowing down, much less stopping. The artist must have wanted to convey the sense that the vertical railroad rails are pointed toward some distant destination, considerably more imposing than this one. How long will the boxcar on the siding have to wait there before a way freight, calling at all the way stations and spur tracks along the line as needed, or perhaps a single mixed train, freight and passengers both, comes along to drop off and collect cars at so quiet a place as this? As for the crossing itself, there is no suggestion of enterprise and activity. It is marginal to the railroad's existence. The weeds and brush have not been cleared away from the tracks any time recently.

The painting is entitled *Where the Southern Cross the Yellow Dog.* The artist is Carroll Cloar (1913–1993). The medium is casein tempera on masonite, and the original hangs in the Memphis Brooks Museum of Art in Tennessee. The title is from a blues song, of which the best-known version is W. C. Handy's "Yellow Dog Blues." I first saw the painting at an exhibition of Southern art at the Virginia Museum of Fine Arts in Richmond. The vividness of the reds, browns, and yellows drew my attention from across the room, and when I walked over to look more closely, the discovery that the subject was a railroad crossing was highly appealing to a longtime train buff. I read the title and was all the more fetched, for I knew the "Yellow Dog Blues" quite well.

In the folk-blues song as adapted by Handy, a man who has found it necessary to leave town in a hurry is sending back word of his whereabouts to a lady friend in Tennessee. "Your Easy Rider," he informs her—the imagery is sexual, as in the opening line, "Ever since Miss Susan Johnson lost her Jockey, Lee"—has fled, having hopped a freight train, "a southbound rattler, side-door Pullman car," and is temporarily resident at the place where the tracks of the Southern Railway cross those of the Yazoo and Mississippi Valley Railroad, known in the Mississippi Delta as "the Dog" or "the Yellow Dog"—that is, he is in the town of Moorhead, Mississippi, well to the south of Memphis in the Mississippi Delta. The Delta is that formed by the confluence of the Yazoo and Mississippi Rivers, which join at Vicksburg, two hundred miles south of Memphis. (It used to be said that the Delta began in the lobby of the Peabody Hotel, in Memphis.)

Handy said that he wrote the "Yellow Dog Blues" after hearing a black musician singing a blues song containing the words of the title at the railroad depot at Tutwiler, Mississippi, in 1903. His version, published first in 1914 and originally styled as a rag instead of blues, has been recorded many times, with the words variously altered by the performers. Bessie Smith recorded it in 1929. Bill Broonzy sang another, more primitive "Yellow Dog Blues" in the 1930s. The version I prefer is Louis Armstrong's, done in the 1960s. There are others; I have versions by Kid Ory, Buster Bailey, Doc Evans, and, rarest of all, the Hollins Hambones.

For many years W. C. Handy lived and worked in Memphis, Tennessee. So did the artist who created the painting, Carroll Cloar, who said he got the idea for it from a suggestion by Shelby Foote, another Memphis resident. Handy was from Alabama, Cloar from Arkansas, and Foote grew up in Greenville, Mississippi, in the Delta not too far from the crossing at Moorhead.

At the turn of the twentieth century there was, briefly, a branch railroad line known as the Yazoo-Delta, and the likelihood is that this was the origin of the nickname Yellow Dog. So Norm Cohen assumes in his book *Long Steel Rail* (1981). The Y-D, after operating independently from 1898 to 1903, was then incorporated into the Yazoo and Mississippi Valley Railroad, which in turn became part of the Illinois Central system.

It has also been argued, by Max Haymes in an informative article on the Internet, that from the outset the Yazoo and Mississippi Valley was the source of the name Yellow Dog, and that a Yazoo-Delta Railroad may never have existed. The term itself, he proposes, refers to a "yellow dog" contract, a type of labor agreement all too prevalent in the South in those times, whereby as a condition of employment a worker agreed not to join a union.

This may well have been, but the nickname *Yellow Dog* for Yazoo-Delta is so obvious, and so in accord with popular practice with railroad names during that era, that it seems more likely that whatever its formal designation, the Yazoo-Delta was what the railroad continued to be called in the area. Not only the nickname but the line from the song were common parlance in the state of Mississippi. The novelist Elizabeth Spencer, who grew up in Carrollton, forty miles east of Moorhead and outside the Delta, tells a story about one of the Bingham boys of that town who was serving as an officer in the American Expeditionary Force in France during World War I. He was supervising the work of a company of black enlisted men, and, far from his native heath and feeling homesick, he called out, "Does anybody here know where the Southern crosses the Yellow Dog?"

"Mo'head, boss!" one soldier responded without hesitation, and the two Mississippians had a reunion then and there. (The same story was in point of fact told about various white and black Mississippians from numerous towns, and may be apocryphal. *Si non è vero, è ben' trovato.*)

In any event, the IC, whose main line between Chicago, Memphis, and New Orleans lay east of the Yazoo River some thirty miles beyond Moorhead, discontinued all service on the branch that had once led north-south between Clarksdale and Yazoo City through Moorhead. As for the crossing's east-west trackage, it was once part of the Southern Railway system, then became the independent Columbus and Greenville, which continues to operate between those two Mississippi cities. Thus the grade crossing at Moorhead is no longer a rail junction, though short lengths of track have been retained north and south for touristic purposes, together with a historical marker and a gazebo for viewing the storied place where the Southern used to cross the Yellow Dog.

Cloar has said that originally the painting was a sketch. The view that the painter selected can be identified from photographs of the crossing as that looking east along the onetime Southern, now the Columbus and Greenville, tracks. The horizontal Yazoo-Delta-Illinois Central rails in the painting, as noted, are presented as if no train could actually travel through the crossing on them, but all of the numerous photographs of the famous crossing itself, some of which may be viewed on the Internet, show gaps in the vertical Southern rails that would allow a train to cross via the horizontal, Yellow Dog tracks. These are not very prominent, however; to spot them one must look carefully.

Did Carroll Cloar knowingly omit the gaps in the tracks, or did he not realize that they were necessary to the working of the rail crossing? I should think the former. Cloar was not engaged in documenting the relative state of maintenance of the two railroad rights-of-way at Moorhead, Mississippi, and neither was he re-creating, for purposes of historical record, a precise, factually accurate image of the details of the railroad crossing. *Where the Southern Cross the Yellow Dog* is an artist's statement. Its impact has palpably to do with one's feelings: it is shaped and formed to embody a mood.

Where are the man and woman walking along the tracks going? Anyone writing a story set at the crossing would have to furnish a destination for them, since fiction, existing as it does in linear time, requires a plot. Nothing in Cloar's painting offers any hint of their destination, other than that it must obviously be close by. On a midautumn day, with the leaves turning but not yet falling from the trees, the weather a little on the coolish side, they are crossing the tracks; that is all.

Other than the fact that it is a grade crossing, what is the relationship, if any, between the scene in the painting itself and the title given it by the artist, or the blues song from which he borrowed it? For that matter, except for the title assigned to it, what reason have we to assume that the scene being portrayed has anything to do with the South?

The names of the railroads in the title, and the reference to the particular song, would indicate that the scene is set in Moorhead, Mississippi. If one looks closely, the name MOORHEAD can be seen painted on the water tower. Still, there are towns of that name in a half-dozen other states, located in the Northeast and Midwest as well as elsewhere in the South. To carry this line of fanciful argument farther, could Carroll Cloar have with equal plausibility entitled this painting "Railroad Crossing in Connecticut"? Would Edward Hopper, say, or John Sloan have painted a scene like this, and in just this way? In other words, is this a *Southern* painting, or a painting with a Southern scene? It is a question that could with equal relevance be posed about Southern fiction and poetry.

Assuredly the artist's technique is not of itself tied in with the American South; it is closer to Seurat than to steamboat gothic or tourist-trade watercolor. It is what the painting portrays, and how it portrays it, that places it in familiar literary territory. Weed-grown roadbeds; a freight car on a siding; a mill of some kind—probably a cotton gin, for there is no grain elevator; a water tower; black people: these are associated with the early- and mid-twentieth-century rural and small-town South, as delineated in many hundreds of Southern novels. The black man and woman are not Picturesque, however, and do not function as Local Color exotics. They are going about their business and look as if they had walked alongside those tracks habitually and often.

The mood of this midautumn day at this grade crossing is not one of anticipation; no train is expected to arrive on these tracks any time soon. Apparently the autumn weather does have nip enough to it to warrant the wearing of coat and sweater, but there is no sense of chill, and certainly not of bleakness. Neither is there excitement or exhilaration; the painting would never do for the cover of an L. L. Bean catalog. If there is a dominant tone to the painting, it is that of Time passing by. I think of lines from a poem by John Crowe Ransom: "Autumn days in our section / Are the most used-up thing on earth."

As noted earlier, this is a whistle-stop, a way station; express trains, manifest freights, do not call here. They roll right through town en route between busier places, and no doubt only a few each day come by at all. Meanwhile everyday life in the community goes on, but at no very ambitious pace. (I am writing about the place as shown in this painting, not Moorhead, Mississippi.) Not until 1981, almost two decades after the artist sketched the crossing, was the Yellow Dog branch abandoned by the Illinois Central and the tracks torn up, leaving only the old Southern Railway trackage in active use. Yet surely the painting, with the weeds growing over the cross ties (which cannot even be seen), the single boxcar on the siding far up the way, the underbrush faded to sere and straw, can be said to foreshadow what will happen, right down to the crossing boards and the gapless vertical rails blocking the use of the horizontal tracks. What the painter's imagination saw there was retrogression. To quote from another poem by John Crowe Ransom, "Declension looks from our land; it is old."

When Cloar went looking for the place where the Southern crossed the Yellow Dog, he was engaged in a historical investigation. Not only did the song itself go back more than a half century into the past, but by 1964 the day of the railroads as the principal means of travel, linking the small towns of the South and the nation to the outside world, was done. There is the sense that the town in the painting, and those who like the man and woman walking alongside the tracks live there, have been left behind.

This visual creation by a painter born in Arkansas, living in Memphis, and drawing upon emotions that are typically associated with the music of the blues, seems bound in with a known, diminished time and place. To quote from another folk song, "Goin' to lay my head on that lonesome railroad line / And let the 2:19 pacify my troublin' mind." Neither the scene chosen, nor the subject matter, the people, the season, the foliage, the time of year, nor the combination of colors—no one of these is unique to the region. Yet their joint presence, their imaginative confluence in a work of art, amounts to what we have learned to recognize and to identify as a characteristic Southern context: in W. C. Handy's formulation, "Ev'ry cross tie, bayou, burg and bog / Way down where the Southern cross' the Dog."

One might call it Regionalism, a term that was popular in the 1930s, but in literary and artistic usage nowadays that would imply limitations, as in "of regional interest"—which when used to describe a new book suggests not so much that the work is grounded in the particulars of an American region as that only the residents of that region would find it of any interest. In that sense Carroll Cloar was certainly no Regionalist.

Neither was a contemporary of Cloar's, Eudora Welty, whose first novel, *Delta Wedding* (1946), begins: "The nickname of the train was the Yellow Dog. Its real name was the Yazoo Delta. It was a mixed train." Unlike her fellow Mississippian William Faulkner, but like Carroll Cloar as a painter, she wrote her books about the extraordinary in the commonplace. Her people are of the everyday sort, and she portrayed, in the seeming ordinariness, the enormous complexity of humans. If you were to see most of her characters—even the major ones, the protagonists—coming along the sidewalk you probably wouldn't think to look twice, and yet as explored in language by Eudora Welty they possess a depth, a meandering but stubbornly maintained complication, that makes them both unique and, finally, mysterious. The same is true of the places, the Mississippi cities and towns that she chronicled and delineated so intricately and often so amusingly. They are little Southern communities, apparently unremarkable, that were shaped by her into the focal point of human existence

Delta Wedding, set in the Delta in September 1923, opens with a little girl, Laura McRaven, traveling aboard the Yazoo-Delta mixed passenger-freight from her home in Jackson, Mississippi, to a small community in the Delta, Fairchilds, where there is to be a wedding at Shellmound plantation. Her mother, who has recently died, was raised there as part of the Fairchild family, who own the several plantations on whose doings the life of the community is centered. The windows in the passenger car are propped open with sticks of kindling wood. Overhead a kerosene lantern swings on a chain. Outside, butterflies can keep pace with the train, which at one point stops so that the engineer can pick some goldenrod. When the Yellow Dog enters the Delta the land, planted in cotton, "was perfectly flat and level but it shimmered like the wing of a lighted dragonfly. It seemed strummed, as though it were an instrument and someone had touched it." Sometimes the train crosses over a bayou atop an iron bridge. As evening comes Laura McRaven watches "the sky, the field, the little track, and the bayou, over and over—all that had been bright or dark was now one color."

Unlike most of the numerous other members of the Fairchild family, stretching back across four generations to pre–Civil War days, nine-year-old Laura already knows, even if she cannot quite articulate it yet, that the universe does not revolve around Shellmound plantation, and that there are places and doings beyond its borders that are real, and that matter: "'My papa has taken me on trips—I know about geography,'" she tells herself. "But in the great confines of Shellmound, no one listened." An intricate, elusive story about a plantation family, with its myths, its alliances, its celebrations and sorrows, *Delta Wedding* chronicles a seemingly closed world, in which a ritualized, ordered family existence goes on, Time and death are ignored, and violence and misery are screened from view. Occasionally these intrude, of course, but for the most part all that is inordinate and disruptive is kept covered, as if Shellmound, and the Fairchilds, and the structured, ritualized community of the Delta, might continue forever.

As for the Yellow Dog, whose tracks and presence wind through the Yazoo country like a leitmotif, it too seems domesticated and harmless. Seemingly gentled and part of the landscape, the steam locomotive and its train of cars nevertheless persist and will not be shunted aside: "The Yellow Dog started up again and came on by, inching by, its engine, with Mr. Doolittle *saluting,* and four cars, freight, white, colored, and caboose, its smoke like a poodle tail curled overhead, an inexcusable sight." If the Fairchilds seem exempt from its potency, not so a strange girl who had been walking up the tracks and was killed. The Fairchild women decline to hear about that. "Change the subject," the news bearer is told. Violent events, immoderate deeds, and rebellious demands are not to be acknowledged. What matters in Fairchilds is whatever suits the needs and wishes of the family. Even so, on several occasions we are reminded that the family's near-feudal domain and wealth are dependent upon a labor system in which the blacks provide the labor, and that they are kept in line, when necessary by violence.

Yet the apparently self-sufficient community, seemingly impervious to time, is not only exposed to the forces of change but, however these may go unnoticed by all but a few family members, is already caught up in the historical process that will inevitably disrupt and dismantle much that is assumed to be permanent and unassailable. Eudora Welty deliberately set her story in a time shortly before the life of the Delta would undergo natural disaster and economic debacle—the devastating flood of 1927, the precipitous tumble in cotton prices that would precede the Great Depression, the migration of black labor to the cities of the Upper South and the Midwest, the erosion of the plantation economy, and the beginnings of what in future decades was to prove a profound transformation of the system of caste and class that had dominated the Delta, the State of Mississippi, and the Deep South for so long.

All that and more is implicit in the portraiture of a Southern place that Eudora Welty created in her novel, and it is not at all a coincidence that the Yellow Dog is so conspicuous throughout. The train is, after all, an instrument of change. For all the little mixed train's seeming diminutiveness and eccentricity, the railroad is how the cotton gets marketed that sustains Shellmound, the Fairchilds, and the Delta economy. The parent road, the Illinois Central, "the main line of mid-America," is no regional curiosity but a powerful, far-flung business enterprise.

Social and historical change is taking place, and it is being resisted, whether at Shellmound plantation or the junction where the tracks cross. *Ut pictura, poesis.* As in painting, so in poetry. Like Carroll Cloar's painting, Eudora Welty's novel is structured in mutability. As Bill Broonzy has it in a more primitive, folk version of "Yellow Dog Blues,"

The Southern cross the Dog at Moorhead, and she keeps on
    through
Yes, the Southern cross the Dog at Moorhead, and she keeps on
    through
If my baby goes to Georgia, believe I'm goin' to Georgia too

In its spring 1958 number, the *Sewanee Review* contained a remarkable essay by Walker Percy, "Metaphor as Mistake." None of his novels had yet been published. The essay, which was later included in his book *The Message in the Bottle* (1975), had to do with the way that a seeming misnaming can sometimes intensify a poetic image.

Percy gave several examples, among them a hawk seen while he was hunting with his father and a black guide in south Alabama. The hawk's flight was straight and swift, then abruptly the bird folded its wings and plummeted into the woods. Greatly impressed, he asked the guide what the bird was called, and was told it was a blue-dollar hawk. When later his father explained to him that the true name was blue-darter hawk, he was disappointed at the correction.* The intensity and vividness of what he had seen and been told by the guide had made a lasting impression on him, and his father's more "accurate" naming, which was materially "correct" where the guide's was "wrong," was considerably less satisfying. "Blue-dollar hawk" not only served as a name for what the boy had seen but also offered an element of mystery, which, because the guide, for that place, time, and function, possessed Authority as a Namer, served to confirm a memorable imaginative experience.

In such a context, Percy declares, the name is neither "right" nor "wrong" as a scientific or logical designation, and neither is it a description of what the bird does. The term proposed by the guide offers an analogy, which, answering the boy's hunger for understanding the cognitive impact of the experience by linking what he has seen with another genuine object, has provided what Percy, citing the poet Gerard Manley Hopkins,

* The hawk in question was very likely a sharp-shinned hawk (*Accipiter striatus*), seen throughout the eastern half of the United States and Canada, known also as the "Little Blue Darter." Alexander Sprunt, Jr., and E. Burnham Chamberlain, *South Carolina Bird Life* (Columbia: University of South Carolina Press, 1949).

describes as Inscape—the apprehended nature of a being. Another word for it might be *Quidditas,* or *Whatness.*

I noted earlier that, as one who was more than casually interested in railroading and trains, I found myself drawn to the painting when I perceived that it depicted a railroad crossing. The same interest led me to note that as a crossing this one was deficient, in that a train could move through it only along one set of tracks. It occurs to me that the process of "Metaphor as Mistake," as Walker Percy's essay describes it, might have something to do with my experience of Carroll Cloar's painting. Was the depiction of the railroad crossroads made more vivid for me, was its emotional impact intensified, *because* of the "error," the tracks that couldn't be crossed by a train? Certainly the perception of that "error" had become part of my experience of seeing the painting. And might it have been that the name Cloar had given to his painting, *Where the Southern Cross the Yellow Dog,* had contributed substantially to my apprehension of it—to my sense of its Inscape?

No artist can communicate a totally new experience to us, whether with images or with words; we can apprehend a work only in terms of what we already know. Prior to encountering Cloar's painting at the Virginia Museum of Fine Arts, I had seen many railroad crossings and photographs of crossings. But the crossing I saw in his painting was more than just another such in a series. It was also a powerful *interpretation,* not only of one such crossing located in Mississippi, but of an *Ur*-crossing, of "*crossing-ness,*" in color, light, and shape; and, as noted earlier, it embodies emotions having to do with time, the seasons, loneliness, declension, destinations, human purposiveness and natural indifference, and so on. The eye of the artist adduced the presence of these qualities, and his craft re-created them.

Just as the guide, by Naming the blue-dollar hawk, not only identified but also confirmed the hawk for the young Walker Percy, so the painter, by means of the authority of his artistry, both informed me of the appearance and certified the emotional dimensions of an experience that was familiar and yet that, until clarified for me through the gift of his imagination, I had not understood in just that way.

My interest in railroads, which without question played a part in my response to the painting, also caused me to notice at once the absence of gaps in the vertical trackage, and later to go looking for photographs to verify their existence in the "real-life" model at Moorhead. The kind of knowledge that the painting imaged for me, however, went considerably deeper than the technical accuracy with which the railroad equipment was reproduced. It was the communicated sense of the vertical tracks as reaching out toward and beyond the horizon that compelled my assent.

Thus the supposed "error" came about in the service of a truth, which involved an emotional perception having to do with the seeming linear inevitability of the progress of the rails through the quiet town, past the mill and the water tower and the boxcar on the siding, up the right-of-way, and toward an imagined convergence beyond the viewer's sight. The "mistake" turned out to enhance the experience of artistic cognition, not because it was either "wrong" or "right" from a technological standpoint, but because noticing it intensified the moment of perception. This is the way it is with the tracks at grade crossings, the painting says.

Or, in the instance of the actual place where the Southern crossed the Yellow Dog, the way it *was*. It should come as something less than a complete surprise that the crossing, *as a crossing*, no longer exists. If you wanted to travel to the Delta now, you couldn't ride there aboard a train. After all, a reminder that weeds will grow up between cross ties, and that all things on earth and in Mississippi come and go in their time, is implicit in the painting, in Eudora Welty's novel, and in the "Yellow Dog Blues."

Four

THOUGHTS ON FICTIONAL PLACES

We tend to see the world in terms of what artists, literary and otherwise, have shown us about it. Lewis Simpson and I were driving once from Oxford to Greenville, Mississippi. When we reached Greenwood and the cantilever bridge over the Yazoo River, painters were at work. At the entrance was a sign:

> BRIDGE BEING PAINTED. STOP ON OTHER SIDE
> TO HAVE PAINT SPOTS REMOVED FROM YOUR CAR

There is no doubt about who taught us to identify the comedy in that: the same author who noticed the sign outside the McLain Bijou theater in *The Golden Apples:*

> DEPOSIT REQUIRED FOR GOING IN TO TALK

Would we have thought of the wording of the paint sign as comic if we had encountered it in Ohio, or Vermont? Hard to say, but doubtless we would not have seen it in quite the same way. It was not the wording of the sign alone, but the mode of looking at people in their time and place that enabled us to view it in other than strictly practical terms. (I don't recall whether any paint was found and removed from the car.)

Elsewhere, one of Eudora Welty's characters remarks that Edna Earle Ponder was the kind of person who could sit for hours wondering how the tail of the first *C* got through the second one in Coca-Cola. Until then

41

I'd never so much as noticed the calligraphy, never thought to speculate that there might be anything to it other than a brand name.

᷍᷍᷍

Thomas Wolfe writes of the far-wandering W. O. Gant riding a streetcar home from the train station in Altamont: "There was a warm electric smell and one of hot burnt steel." Growing up in Charleston, South Carolina, I rode a trolley car downtown and back six days a week, but not until I encountered *Look Homeward, Angel* did I recognize the experience as visually and sensorily remarkable. I have since written about the looks and odors of trolley cars and trains; Wolfe showed me how to observe them emotionally, or, more accurately, made me realize that I did observe them emotionally.

᷍᷍᷍

Emotional experience is three-dimensional; all places in fiction are potentially sensory. Wolfe used lots of adjectives to re-create his feelings; Ernest Hemingway, very few. When young, in the first creative-writing class I taught, I was once pontificating about the supposed lack of descriptive adjectives in Hemingway's prose. One of my students, John Barth, disagreed. "The yellow overcoats in 'The Killers' are the only ones I can remember in fiction," he said.

Hemingway agreed with Mark Twain on the deployment of the adjective: "when in doubt, strike it out." William Faulkner did not; early in the unfolding first sentence of *Absalom, Absalom!* he depicts Quentin Compson listening to Miss Rosa Coldfield as she drones away about events that happened long before he was born. The time is a "long still hot weary dead September afternoon"; the place is the parlor of Miss Rosa's long-unpainted house. The adjectives describe the climate, tell us how Quentin feels about the place and the occasion, and begin to suggest what kind of person young Quentin is.

Neither Hemingway nor Clemens could have written anything so emotionally intricate as *Absalom, Absalom!* Neither would have wished to. "Well, you better not think about it," Nick Adams is advised at the end of "The Killers." But Faulkner could not have written about his native

place without thinking about the complexity of Quentin's emotions concerning it.

~~~

Clemens wrote about the South during the heyday of Local Color, the
later nineteenth century. Reading Local Color fiction got him to depict-
ing his early days in a town fronting on the Mississippi River: "After all
these years I can picture that old time to myself now, just as it was then."
What he did not do was stop at the level of descriptive portraiture that
his magazine contemporaries did, with the surface oddities and quaint-
nesses of the place of his birth and rearing. Sam Clemens had strong, sometimes contradictory feelings about the country of his early experience; his
literary gift compelled him, inevitably if sporadically, to ferret them out.
Physical description deepened into moral vision.

~~~

Back before television destroyed the market for magazine fiction the
publications for would-be writers used to run advertisements for decks of
cards showing plot situations. The faces of the cards were divided into three
sections, each with the segment of a plot. You shuffled the deck, dealt yourself three cards, and by combining the top section of one, the middle section of another, and the bottom section of a third, you had yourself the
beginning, middle, and end of a story to write. All you needed to do was
to fill in the details—that is, provide some texture for the story's structure, such as the place where it would happen. The European Formalist
Vladimir Propp would very likely have agreed with the approach.

~~~

Anthony Powell's magnificent *A Dance to the Music of Time* takes place
for the most part in and around London. There is comparatively little
physical description of the place itself, yet the comic quartet, each made
up of three novels, seems not merely English but inescapably Londonish
in nature. One can scarcely imagine Powell's narrator—or for that matter
Powell himself—living in Westchester County or the West Side of Man-
hattan Island, not to say Nashville, Tennessee.

Obviously it is not the particulars of the metropolitan geography, but the way the characters comport themselves in it and what the author thinks is significant about their behavior and what is not, that establish the place and its moral identity. I say this without the local knowledge to spot any of the real-life models. But any British litterateur could—which is to the point; for the fiction grows out of, though it does not depend for readability upon, just that kind of familiarity.

The nearest equivalent in this country is, I suppose, New York City. Alfred Kazin once quoted the response of Philip Rahv when told that one of the habitual contributors to the *Partisan Review* had published a novel: "Who's in it?" But American novelists for the most part don't write *about* New York City to anything like the extent to which British novelists do about Oxford, London, and environs. For one thing, it isn't necessary to live or die in New York City; an occasional professional visit will suffice.

~~~

The Great Theme of Henry James, the contrast of cultures inherent in the American presence in Europe, is predicated upon the emotional dimensions of place. In London, Paris, Venice, Rome are the institutions of history and high culture that make possible the full and ample exercise of the artistic imagination. Accompanying them, seemingly inseparable from them, are the fixed restrictions of rank and class. Enter Christopher Lambert Adam, the New Man, innocent of those stratifications, having come into his adult strength and gone abroad in pursuit of the fruits of European culture. Can he put on that knowledge with his power?

If that American arriviste is a materialist, a sensualist, a cad, or else if he is so morally frozen as to be hopelessly rigid, nothing will happen beyond the exchange of money for the superficial trappings of culture. But if, when tested in the European social crucible, that American, while remaining morally incorruptible, proves receptive toward new experiences, he (or she) can win through to genuine artistic enlightenment, and henceforth be One of Those upon Whom Nothing Is Lost. So the European place is the proving ground for aesthetic and moral vision—as in that early Jamesean parable of the American artist, "Daisy Miller," Winterbourne being the one who flunks the test, even as Lambert Strether later passes it in *The Ambassadors.*

One would be hard put, in James's international fiction, to turn up much evidence for the possibility of the artistic vision being fulfilled while in residence in the United States. His famous catalog of the institutions customarily used in the exercise of that vision, but unavailable to the American literary sensibility—"no sovereign, no court, no personal loyalty, no aristocracy," and so forth—was developed to explain the poverty of social texture in Hawthorne's fiction. The assumption on which James proceeds is that artistic life in America will be at worst crass and materialistic, and at best thin and undernourished. "American humor" (he places the term within quotation marks), based as it is on the chasm between reality and aspiration, alone may flourish there.

The outrage among the intellectual set on either side of the Charles River that followed publication of *The Bostonians,* in which James satirized the frazzled remnants of New England Transcendentalism—reformers, do-gooders, spirit rappers, simpletons in general—may well have been perceived by him as validation of the wisdom of his own decision to depart the American scene for Europe. Yet James's view of Europe, as is often pointed out, is not really of Paris, London, Venice, Rome, but of Americans visiting in those cities.

Late in his life, after long years of self-induced exile, he comes home to survey the American scene and is appalled by the vulgarity and the commercialism. The despoilment of the continent is producing an abiding ugliness. When there is vitality, as in immigrant-crowded New York City, it is alien to the older America of his childhood. What elegance exists is essentially that of a commercial hotel. *The American Scene* may be said to adumbrate Pudd'nhead Wilson's aphorism: "*October 12, the Discovery.* It was wonderful to find America, but it would have been even more wonderful to miss it."

When I reread James's chapters on New York City recently, I thought of Alfred Kazin's memoir *A Walker in the City.* From James's standpoint, it would be almost inconceivable that Kazin's work could ever have been written. Yet between James's despairing visit to New York City, and the childhood in Brownsville that Kazin describes so beautifully, scarcely twenty-five years intervened.

At the opposite extreme from Henry James on the American urban scene is the description of Fitzgerald and Moy's in *Sister Carrie:* "It was a truly swell saloon." I doubt that James had read Dreiser's first novel at the time, but the adverb and adjective alone would have confirmed all of his apprehensions about what vulgar things were happening to the English language in the turn-of-the-century United States. Certainly when James was a boy living in Washington Square in the pre–Civil War years, nobody who was writing novels would have chosen to describe a tavern—it would not have been called a saloon—in just this way. By the early 1900s much had changed; the scope of the American novel had been broadened to include varieties of experience, some of them unpleasing, and attitudes toward it, that even a professional realist such as William Dean Howells considered too crude to be written about. Yet the true vulgarian of the day was not Theodore Dreiser, a great literary artist in his own right; it was William Sidney Porter (O. Henry).

Sister Carrie was published in 1900; *The Ambassadors,* in 1903. A century later, and who is now the champion active vulgarian? What are the top ten paperback novels currently on sale at the Raleigh-Durham Airport?

～ฅ)

The use of locale in a best-selling "blockbuster" novel such as James Michener's *Hawaii* differs from its presence in Eudora Welty's Mississippi or, to choose a more recent example, Lee Smith's Appalachia, in that Michener's people are imposed upon the place from without, while Welty's and Smith's people grow out of an emotional relationship to the place and are manifestations of the imaginative experience of the locales in their creators' own lives.

In the best fiction, place is not only geography and history; it is a way of looking at the world. In that sense, the imagination that created "The Killers" is as surely a product of the city of Chicago as is that of *Sister Carrie,* even though Dreiser set out consciously to write about the geographical and historical entity of the place in its time, while Hemingway had no such objective.

～ฅ)

In the early decades of the nineteenth century it was considered appropriate to have actual historical characters play prominent parts in the plots of period romances. We have since become more scrupulous about keeping the documentary record and the fictional action separate. The contemporary historical novel customarily portrays historical figures, but does not let them participate importantly in the fictional plot.

The exception would be novels such as E. L. Doctorow's *Ragtime,* which dissolve fact into fiction in order to play games with "reality." These succeed as fiction, however, for only so long as we remember that what is going on *is* the deliberate blurring of known history and novelistic fantasy. So-called metafiction can be sustained only *as* illusion. Without a generally agreed upon reality that can be violated, it would make little sense. Barth's *The Sot-Weed Factor* rings the changes on appearances versus reality, with the illusions securely grounded in (and afloat upon) the geography and early history of the Chesapeake Bay country.

But writers of "metafiction" are not the only authors who sometimes enjoy playing games with time and place. In *The Last Gentleman,* Walker Percy has Will Barrett remember being introduced as a child to Senator Oscar W. Underwood of Alabama. Later Barrett discovers that the senator died before he was born. The youthful introduction could well have happened to Barrett's creator, however, and very likely did.

Hamilton Basso, in *The View from Pompey's Head,* opens with a man aboard a Pullman car, arriving home in the Southern coastal city of his birth and raising. The train backs into the station, from which the man is conveyed to a downtown hotel. When I first read it I was sure that the author was describing the advent of the morning Palmetto Limited at Union Station in Charleston, South Carolina. The geographical arrangements seemed to fit. Reviewers of Basso's novel, however, located it variously in Savannah, Jacksonville, and New Orleans, where the author grew up. With the reader as willing collaborator, seemingly specific details could be made to suggest all of those places.

A little readerly empathy is a treacherous thing. As Stephen Dedalus said, "Local colour. Work in all you know. Make them accomplices."

The novelist might be said to be in the position of the little boy found standing at the corner. "I'm running away from home," he explained, "but my mother won't let me cross the street by myself." However faithfully—or sketchily—a work of fiction may draw upon the material of geography and history, it is based on illusion. Depending upon attitudes, objectives, and assumptions about the needs of life and art, novelists labor to imitate "reality": in other words, to re-create it in language. A novel that doesn't happen somewhere is a contradiction in terms. It needn't, of course, be a known geographical entity; the interior of a spaceship will do. The novelist can leave it up to the reader to furnish almost all the trapping and fixings. But to adopt the punch line of another joke, "Well, everybody's got to be somewhere."

~⁀⁌

There are novelists—to a degree John Barth is one, James Joyce another—for whom fiction must not only happen in a known, bounded place, but the details of the place itself must be authentic. What prompts this kind of insistence upon authenticity of detail is something beyond an effort to insure a continued suspension of disbelief on the reader's part. At least as important, in writing fiction the novelist is engaged in doing an audacious thing: creating fictional life out of language, inventing entire characters, endowing them with *consciousness*—and doing this in a very precisely delineated setting, against which the authenticity of the fictional characters can be readily measured. It is not enough that Leopold Bloom, Stephen Dedalus, Molly Bloom, and the others be made to live in Dublin; they must be *of* Dublin. It is something like building a bridge, or creating a platform that will reach out from a recognizable, substantial place into what until then has been empty air. To undergird the span as it extends into the void, the novelist needs the moral support of pilings that will help to stabilize his projection in the here and now—needs it for his own self-confidence perhaps most of all.

Desmond McCarthy had a story about someone visiting Joyce's apartment in Paris. On one wall was a print showing Nora Joyce's home city of Cork. When the guest looked at it closely, he realized that the frame was constructed of cork. You have no idea how difficult it was to secure that frame, Joyce remarked, adding that of course it was essential to find it. His prodigious imagination required buttressing on more than one level of authenticity.

This was the author who, when *Finnegans Wake* was criticized as being trivial, replied that it was not only trivial but quadrivial.

~⁓

It would be interesting to know the books of reference, maps, and other such material that various novelists kept close at hand when they wrote certain books. Joyce kept a goodly supply of Dubliniana, including city directories, almanacs, rail and trolley car schedules, street maps, programs of fairs and bazaars, church registers, and the like. By contrast, I doubt that William Faulkner required a great deal of local documentation; he was the kind of writer who could have Quentin Compson commit suicide by jumping into the Charles River in June of 1910 in one novel, and in another have him leave Mississippi for Harvard the following September. But he knew where everything was, and had been, in his little "postage-stamp's worth" of north Mississippi.

Sometimes it helps for readers to see the originals of the places of fiction. What is striking about Rowan Oak, Faulkner's home in Oxford, Mississippi, is that the exterior, with its columns and portico, looks like the abode of a General Compson, but the interior seems more that of a Flem Snopes.

I wrote my own three novels with a city map and a chart of Charleston harbor close by. In retrospect I believe that what I should have used instead was a stethoscope.

~⁓

It has been my experience that novelists tend to be able to appreciate and to admire work composed out of artistic assumptions very different from their own. Poets generally do not. This may be because by definition the writing of fiction requires the novelist to come to terms with the documentation of the world. Poets, by contrast, seem to be engaged in a war with it; they wish to intensify it beyond its particularities, "like gold to airy thinnesse beat," and each poem is a field of action. All other contemporary poets are either allies or enemies; there are no neutrals.

It is useful and valuable training for would-be novelists to try a hand at writing poems. It is also appropriate for most of them to give it up after a time. Thomas Hardy is the—or maybe *an*—exception that proves the rule.

Just as in answer to the advent of photography the French Impressionists concentrated on portraying the nuances and emphases of light, which the photographic plate couldn't capture, so one response of the novelist to movies and television has been to explore the subtleties of consciousness. There are intricacies of characterization in *The Golden Apples,* infused into fictional locale and reinforced by myth, that go far beyond what any photographic lens, however sensitive, can reproduce. Language may not be our sole knowable "reality," as some claim, but it is as close as we can come to identifying and embodying its workings in time and place, and the tension between the apparent and the real is the terrain where the literary artist works. "October rain on Mississippi fields, maybe on the whole South, for all she knew on the everywhere. She stared into its magnitude." That is Virgie Rainey at the close of Eudora Welty's best book of all. What her vision notices is what we can thereafter recognize for ourselves. And that, I believe, is where we came in.

Five

QUESTIONS OF INTENT: SOME
THOUGHTS ON AUTHOR-SHIP

Authorial intent—what the writer of fiction has in mind to do when setting out to tell a story—can be a tricky business. It is not simply a matter of thinking up a plot and writing it out. The story may not go where the author intends for it to go, or turn out to mean what he thought he was writing.

No two writers set about writing fiction in exactly the same way. Some try to plan everything out in advance; others proceed from sentence to sentence and paragraph to paragraph, as the spirit moves. Some develop chapter-by-chapter synopses, to which they may or may not pay any heed once they begin writing. And so on. I propose to ruminate on the subject of authorial intention, using for fodder my own fiction and that of my betters.

By no means is storytelling a completely rational undertaking. To imagine and to understand the thoughts and actions of the characters, writers must draw upon their own experience, adapting, postulating, incorporating, and reshaping as they go. Openly and by intent they make use of what they know, including what they feel, and the recognition and understanding of one's own motivations and responses, much less of anyone else's, can be an imperfect affair.

Because as writers we not only permit our emotional experience to become involved but positively insist upon it, in the course of telling stories we may discover that what we really think about something or someone differs from what we had until then supposed. Our conscious assumptions and beliefs can turn out to be at loggerheads with our inmost feelings.

The uncovering of our own emotions can be startling, even disturbing, and we may seek to deny or disguise what we find out. Writers whose conscious intentions may struggle against where their imagination has taken them may insist, to themselves and to others, that what they have written doesn't say what it appears to say. This is what D. H. Lawrence meant when he cautioned the reader of fiction always to trust the tale, not the artist.

In dreams, one object—a person, a place, a situation—substitutes itself for another, and thereby calls our attention to resemblances and connections that we hadn't previously perceived. Freed from the "real-life" boundaries of time, distance, and logical consistency, our imagination will work out patterns while we are asleep that our waking thoughts may not have uncovered.

Something like that is what can happen when we set out to write fiction. We might call it the Re-creative Impulse, the urge, or the compulsion, to recombine the ingredients of our experience in order to display and understand them. Coleridge termed it the Esemplastic Power. I do not mean to imply that this can happen only when we write fiction or poetry. As a genre and as a creative process, however, fiction, like poetry, encourages it, and indeed counts on it happening.

How the literary imagination functions, the degree to which it reshapes and reforms its materials as it goes along, the extent to which a story can be thought through and its developments sketched out in advance— these vary from writer to writer and from work to work. What seems clear is that there is no one right or wrong way to plan and write a story.

On the other hand, neither do novelists start writing from scratch, not even those who persist in using ink pens. They may not all go about the task in the careful, deliberate fashion of Henry James. Neither might they begin the way that Theodore Dreiser says he did for his first novel. Dreiser claimed that on a day in 1899 he took out a sheet of yellow paper, wrote a random title on it, SISTER CARRIE, then started in. Surely a great deal of thinking and supposing had been taking place before Dreiser began describing Carrie Meeber's train trip to Chicago. Equally obviously, Henry

James's muse had its own ways of nudging an intense creative imagination along unpredicted paths.

Perhaps the most familiar case of avowed authorial intent is Edgar Poe's "The Philosophy of Composition," in which he makes an elaborate effort to show that "The Raven" was the product of a totally conscious, abstract decision to compose a poem, and that every line and item in it was a contrived, rational performance. (This is the essay in which Poe wrote that the death of a beautiful woman was unquestionably the most poetical of all topics.) The question, of course, is why the author was intent upon denying any personal emotional involvement in his poem.

It is all very well, when disputes about an author's intentions arise, to insist that it is the written-down story that should command our attention as readers, and that questions about what the author may have intended to do, what his literary models may have been, or what may have been going on in his own personal life or that of his community at the time ought not make the least difference to us.

Why, however, do people go to hear novelists give readings and talk about their work? Why do they wish to know what kind of person it is who wrote the fiction? What can account for their interest in the creative process that produced it? Why are literary biographies written and published, and why do readers buy and read them? Is no more than idle curiosity involved?

I think not. Certainly the story itself is where everything begins (and, ultimately, ends) for the reader. What happens, however, is that readers of fiction, caught up in the telling of a tale, are drawn into the imaginative orbit of the teller. They become interested in how and why the author wrote what they have been reading. Assuredly the reader of a good novel is no purist. The literary theorist, like the passionate trout fisherman discoursing upon the presentation of artificial flies, may hold forth on what is and is not the proper way to go about reading a novel, yet the very nature of the fictional imagination itself invites complicated responses. For just that reason, authorial intentions become of interest to us.

In attempting to understand what authors are up to in their stories, it is important to keep in mind that both conscious and unconscious intention can be involved. One reason novelists write is to discover what the stories may mean. They may not necessarily understand the full meanings in advance, or even be aware of the presence of all the dimensions in their stories. The literary imagination can function on several levels simultaneously, without the writer realizing the implications.

It can be difficult sometimes to accept the fact that because something is *there* in the text of a novel, its existence may not always mean that the novelist consciously and intentionally put it there. American literature scholars are familiar with the letter that Herman Melville wrote to Sophia Hawthorne, expressing his amazed delight at Nathaniel Hawthorne's allegorical reading of *Moby-Dick.* "I had some vague idea while writing it," Melville declared, "that the whole was susceptible of an allegorical construction, and also that the *parts* of it were—but the specialty of many of the particular subordinate allegories, were first revealed to me after reading Mr. Hawthorne's letter."

Unfortunately, Hawthorne's letter about *Moby-Dick* has not survived. But how could Melville possibly have meant what he was saying—that not only the "Spirit Spout" episode, which Mrs. Hawthorne cited to him, but other episodes such as the whiteness of the whale, the quarterdeck, the fire-baptism, the doubloon, the masthead, and all that host of emblematic passages with which Melville's novel is laced, right down to the floating coffin that saves Ishmael at the close, could have been placed there other than by thoroughly conscious authorial intention? More than one interpreter of *Moby-Dick* has found this hard to credit.

Anyone who has written much fiction, however, would probably have no trouble with the assertion. The imagination can come up with some odd congruences; it does not cease functioning once the author has decided where he wants his story to go.

I can illustrate this with something from my own experience as a writer, which had it not happened to me I would find great difficulty in believing could not have been the result of conscious intention. In my novel *The Golden Weather* (1961), set in Charleston, South Carolina, I had a character who was a local poetaster. I wanted him to have written a local-color effusion, the kind that used to be known as a "winged lyric," made up of quaint images of some of the more obviously picturesque features of the Carolina Lowcountry around Charleston. So I set out to write one for him:

MARSH GRASS

It is a carpet, gay in green and gold,
For clouds to sleep upon at high noonday,
As if some Persian merchant-god unrolled
A prayer rug there, then wandered far away.

Now herons weave the corners to the land,
And river currents curl about its side,
Till what was loomed and turned at Samarkand
Is raveled by the turning of the tide.

In coming up with those immortal stanzas, all that I was trying to do was to contrive a typical local-color poem, one that this particular kind of resident poetaster might well have written, making use of materials dear to the Chamber of Commerce. Who, however, is that "Persian merchant-god" who unrolls a "prayer rug" in the marsh around Charleston? Not only the Persians, but the Jews as well, came originally from the Middle East. The protagonist of my novel is named Omar Kohn—Omar the Tent-Maker, but Kohn, a Jewish name. Typically the Jews who came from Europe to settle in the South were merchants, often peddlers.

The carpet that this merchant-peddler-divinity has deposited there is being woven into the marsh grass, made into a part of the local scene. What originated in the Near East as a religious device is being raveled by the tide—which is to say, losing that older religious and racial identity.

In short, what was intended to be a poem "about" the salt marsh around Charleston is at the same time a poem "about" racial and cultural assimilation. Yet not until several years after the novel was published did it occur to me, upon a rereading, that my little manufactured-for-the-occasion lyric in fact encapsulated one of the most deeply felt concerns of my life.

Again, if I had not written the poem myself, it would be hard to convince me that the imagery was not consciously placed there by the author in order to enforce the underlying direction of the novel. How could it *not* have been? Yet no such analogy ever once entered into my calculations when I was writing the book.

Do not misunderstand: the thematic analogy *is* there, and not by chance, either. But it got there not through conscious authorial design, but because such creative imagination as I possessed was dictating the seem-ingly arbitrary choice of imagery. So I for one can readily credit Melville's assertion about the allegory in *Moby-Dick*. To cite another remark by Ishmael in that narrative, "O Nature, and O soul of man! how far beyond all utterances are your linked analogies."

A novelist is likely to find out, once into the writing of a novel, that his characters, and the situations in which they become involved, tend to develop their own dynamics and momentum, and that preconceived plans may have to be adjusted accordingly. This can work negatively as well as positively. In *Moby-Dick* Melville originally planned to do something with a character named Bulkington, but appears to have realized after a time that the story wasn't working out that way. Under similar circumstances his friend Hawthorne would doubtless have eliminated the character entirely; he is scarcely essential to the plot. Instead, Melville, who was given to producing the kind of novels that Henry James termed "loose baggy monsters," composed an apotheosis, as he called it, to Bulkington, and thereafter no more was heard of him.

Suppose, however, that a novelist, having worked out an intricately plotted design for the story he wishes to tell, becomes so intent upon his preconceived plan that he neglects to adapt all his characters to it as he goes along? The difficulties that can arise out of this kind of authorial intention can be illustrated in perhaps the finest political novel ever writ-ten by an American author, Robert Penn Warren's *All the King's Men*.

Red Warren was a prolific, multitalented man, who wrote distinguished fiction, poetry, drama, historical commentary, journalism, and some highly influential literary criticism. He was a dedicated teacher; the textbooks that he and Cleanth Brooks wrote and compiled, notably *Understanding Poetry* (1938), helped shape a generation's approach to reading, and their impact continues to be felt. As a reader and critic Warren was known for the lati-tude of his literary sympathies; his tastes were not narrow or overfastidious.

All the King's Men, his third novel, is not the kind of artistic work that emerged full-blown from its creator's head, in the way that Athena allegedly did from Zeus's. In writing fiction, that can indeed happen sometimes, although not so often as is claimed, and whether for better or for worse. Not, however, with a venturesome author like Warren. He began the novel as a verse play, and not until the third draft, when he decided to redo it as a prose narrative, did a first-person narrator emerge as both the register of the story's meaning and a leading participant in it. It is a measure of the author's adaptability and his readiness to face up to the implications of his technique that Jack Burden, who Warren has described as an accident of the storytelling, could not only take over the narration but also enhance the story's range and moral significance.

Warren once wrote an excellent essay on Joseph Conrad, in which he commented on the way that for the Philosophical Novelist the urge to explore the documentation of the world also becomes the urge to shape it into meanings. The danger inherent in such a tendency is that the fictional elements—the characters, events, settings—can be subordinated to the thematic patterning. In just that way Warren's own formidable conceptual powers, which are of exemplary use to him in his critical essays, sometimes impinge upon his storytelling instincts.

Is it likely that the character in the novel known as Anne Stanton, Jack Burden's childhood girlfriend, as developed in the opening chapters of the story, would ever be drawn physically to the character known as Willie Stark, as likewise developed in the novel, so as to become his mistress? From all that we have seen and been told of her up until then, when it occurs in the story my initial reaction was to find it hard to credit. It seemed to me, and it still does, that Anne Stanton turns to The Boss at that juncture not so much because her own ideals have been shattered by what Jack Burden discovers about her father, as because the design of Warren's story requires her to do it in order to set up the events that will cause Willie's death. The development of the novelist's plot structure, worked out to illustrate and embody Warren's thesis on the nature of human complicity, overrode his feeling for characterization.

Still, when all is said and done, the sweep of the story's working out is powerful enough to bear us along with it. The cast of vividly realized characters and the panoramic presentation of a human community in confrontation with the moral imperatives that arise in response to social change compel our attention. The rise and fall of Willie Stark, country boy, politico, pragmatist, thwarted idealist, tragic hero, as chronicled and interpreted by Jack Burden, remains one of the more memorable creations of American fiction.

In others of Warren's novels, however, a divergence between thematic design and imaginative characterization does considerably more damage. Beginning with his first novel, *Night Rider,* and continuing at least through *At Heaven's Gate, World Enough and Time,* and *Band of Angels,* with the single exception of *All the King's Men* the dramatic conflict between the characters in every instance tends to resolve itself emotionally well before the preconceived plot is allowed to work itself out. In particular *World Enough and Time* goes on and on, far beyond the emotional resolution, because of the author's insistence on his schematic design.

I don't mean to imply that only those novelists who, as did Warren, worked extensively at criticism are likely to be guilty of allowing thematic considerations to tyrannize over the instinct for dramatic construction. No one ever accused William Faulkner of being addicted to the practice of conceptual philosophizing. Yet what can be said of Nancy Mannigoe's murdering Gowan Stevens and Temple Drake's infant child in *Requiem for a Nun,* other than that it is a dreadfully unconvincing way to rescue a faltering marriage? And surely the existence of a sizable portion of *A Fable* can be explained only because at that particular juncture in his career its author's genius as a storyteller succumbed to the urge to hold forth on Mankind. Sometimes even good Homer nods.

I have suggested that a reader's interest in the author of a novel comes about through having been caught up in the personality of the storyteller. By this I have in mind not the role of a first-person narrator, if any, such as Jack Burden in *All the King's Men* or Ishmael in *Moby-Dick,* but the sense that the reader has of being in the company of the storyteller himself, whose presence in the tale is a dimension of the novel. When we read *Huckleberry Finn,* for example, the high point of the story comes when Huck determines to steal Jim out of captivity, even though he will assuredly be consigned to Hell for doing it. The reader knows that it is only because Huck has been reared in a slaveholding society that he thinks that by obeying the promptings of his heart he will be violating a moral law.

Who tells the reader that? Not the first-person narrator, Huck, but the storyteller: Mark Twain. He doesn't say so directly, in so many words, but nonetheless he is intent upon our realizing it; and he communicates it to us through his attitude, his context, his characterizations, the language his people use, and so on. The company of Mark Twain is a palpable and essential component of the novel. So is that of Melville in *Moby-Dick,* of Henry James in *The Ambassadors,* and indeed of the authorial tellers of all successful fiction. Moreover, that presence isn't necessarily the "real-life," biographical author as such, the one whose name appears in the copyright notice, but his projected, created personality as an author. He is part of the story: the teller *in* the tale.

Communicating this personality is an aspect of how fiction is written. It may done with conscious intention, as with Samuel Langhorne Clemens, who liked to be known as Mark Twain in print and on the platform; but, more important, it is an automatic process, the omnipresence of the author of the novel.

The problem with authorial intention of this kind arises when the story-telling presence in the story attempts to contradict the thrust of the narra-tive itself. We do not mind the author, whether overtly or, as in *Huckleberry Finn,* through inference, addressing himself directly to us; on the contrary, we welcome him. What that author cannot get away with, however, is de-claring that his story means one thing while showing it as meaning an-other thing. That, we say, constitutes "authorial intrusion." Instead of the authorial voice being part of the story, it becomes an interruption, even an impediment. It gets in the way of the reader's experience of the fiction. We begin to doubt the storyteller's *authority;* we sense the presence of the "real-life," biographical author trying to manipulate our responses to what he has written. He calls attention to himself at the expense of his own story.

Instances of this sometimes turn up in the fiction of Ernest Heming-way, whose stylistic craftsmanship is so pellucid that the slightest off-note can endanger its credibility. There are times, particularly in Hemingway's later work, when he takes to projecting himself as an Old Pro, possessed of the true *afición* in certain activities, typically those of an outdoors nature such as hunting, fishing, war, boxing, bullfighting, and so on. He communicates word of this status to us through devices such as demon-strations of the self-conscious use of technical nomenclature, or by having a viewpoint character, when in the company of genuine Professionals, share an attitude of superiority toward the untutored and uninformed. A lesser Hemingway novel such as *To Have and Have Not* or *Across the River and into the Trees* is pervaded by this tendency, which in the latter can verge upon the ridiculous.

It was Hemingway's custom, even outright compulsion, to dramatize his own personality, both in his life and in his art. Not surprisingly he was a highly and openly competitive person, given to describing his literary career in terms of rivalry with other authors, and also with some kind of vague but insidious entity known as Them—critics, reviewers, doubters, scoffers, and skeptics in general: "How do you like it now, gentlemen?" This is one reason his biography can be so interesting, and it is only fair to point out that this communicated sense of the author as protagonist can often enliven what he writes.

He could not disguise his feelings, which is both his strength and his limitation. When he sought to deal with abstract ideas he was apt to fall on his face, but no one was ever better as a portrayer of sensuous experience.

So if the matter of authorial intention is sometimes a complex and subtle affair, the example of Ernest Hemingway is as good a way as any to conclude a discussion of it. What does come across when we read his fiction is not so much the Old Pro that he thought he wanted to convince us was writing it, but the gifted and courageous literary artist who was telling it.

Never think that was easy to do.

Six

BLOOM'S LEAP: OR, HOW
FIRM A FOUNDATION

My guess is that anyone who has ever done any serious writing of fiction will willingly testify that there are important differences between how one goes about it and how one might proceed when preparing an essay or a biography. The writer's involvement with the subject is of a different sort, and notwithstanding recent critical theory to the contrary, so too will be the reader's.

I wish to put forward a case for what I perceive as a fundamental distinction between fiction and nonfiction, no matter how well or imaginatively the latter is written, and to maintain that, however the ingredients of one may involve the other, the purposes for which those ingredients are used essentially differ.

Now it is quite true that other kinds of writing can be, to an extent even must be, "imaginative," and equally it is self-evident that even the most fanciful, nonfactual writing involves some documentation. When Yeats, for example, writes of a chestnut tree as a "great rooted blossomer," part of what he has in mind is to represent a tangible, factually identifiable object in language. Equally the instruction sheet to an electric train set that I bought for my grandson begins with the following sentence: "Proper lubrication is important BUT IT MUST NOT BE OVERDONE," which neither in content nor in punctuation is a merely descriptive, factual denotation. Whoever wrote the instructions was expressing an emotion.

One of the problems we encounter when we attempt to think about fiction is that any such analysis must be, in intent at least, logical. We must break down the novel being examined into its component parts. In so doing it is not too difficult to isolate a passage, or a scene, or even a chapter of a work of fiction and to demonstrate that it involves the factual presentation of an observable, even measurable subject—which is to say that, taken in isolation, it is nonfiction. But when we read the novel we do not encounter the passage in isolation; we experience it in a context. And it is the context, the overall engagement with the story, that determines our response.

An essential difference between fiction and nonfiction, it seems to me, has to do with emotion—the way it is employed, the way in which the novelist shapes our involvement as readers. The matter can be gotten at if we consider an episode involving James Joyce. At one point when Joyce was putting the final touches to *Ulysses* he sent a letter to his aunt in Dublin, asking her to go by No. 7 Eccles Street and let him know whether an ordinary man could scale the iron fence out front and drop down to the ground without undue difficulty. He had seen it done once, he told her, but by a young man of athletic build.

Anyone familiar with the novel will at once recognize the allusion, for when Leopold Bloom, who is made to reside at that address, takes the young Stephen Dedalus home for a cup of "Epps's massproduct, the creature cocoa" (*Ulysses,* 1961 Modern Library edition, 677) after Stephen's disastrous adventures in Nighttown, he has forgotten the key to the front door and must climb over the fence, lower himself to the ground, and let himself into the house through the basement.

It is after midnight. The day has been long and trying. Arriving at No. 7 Eccles Street in company with the young Stephen Dedalus, eager to continue his conversation with him, Bloom finds that he has left the front-door key in another pair of trousers—a emblematic act, for ever since the death of their infant son some years ago he has been unwilling and unable to make love to his wife, Molly. He has misplaced the "arruginated male key" to his marriage, and he is in danger of losing Molly, who has that very afternoon committed adultery, rumors to the contrary notwithstanding, for the first time. A strong-willed woman, Molly Bloom may be said to wear the pants in that particular household. But, as the culmination of the events of that day and night of June 16–17, 1904, Bloom will make up his mind to reassert his husbandhood (as Molly wishes him to do) and, one hopes, will thereafter be "keyless" no longer.

So Bloom's leap over the fence will matter a great deal to him—and, to the extent that we are with him in spirit as he aspires to rectify the domestic situation at No. 7 Eccles Street, to the reader as well. In another and larger sense, however, likewise important to the meaning of *Ulysses,* Bloom and all men (and women) remain keyless as to the ultimate meanings of their existence within the universe.

Joyce had the kind of mind in which small things are made to add up, as the persistence of keys in the events of *Ulysses* indicates. Bloom, who is an advertising salesman, spends part of the day searching for an illustration for a newspaper advertisement that will feature the crossed keys of the Manx parliament. And Stephen Dedalus, too, the future novelist but at that date still very much the artist manqué, has handed over the key to the bay-front Martello tower where he has been living with Buck Mulligan. He cannot go home—to the tower, to his family, to his rightful place as Irish artist. The writing of the novel he plans (not *Ulysses* but the equivalent of *A Portrait of the Artist as a Young Man*) will require ten years of self-assumed exile on the continent. He too is still without the key that will unlock the resources of his art (the final words of Joyce's last book, *Finnegans Wake,* are: "The keys to. Given. A way a last a lone a loved a long the").

According to Joyce's friend J. F. Byrne, in *Silent Years: An Autobiography with Memoirs of James Joyce and Our Ireland* (1953), when in 1909 Joyce returned briefly to Ireland from Trieste, he visited Byrne at No. 7 Eccles Street. They went out for a walk, and upon returning Byrne realized that he had left his housekey in the trousers in his bedroom. So he vaulted over the fence railing, dropped down several feet into the front area, entered through the basement, and let Joyce in through the front door.

Byrne, who served as a model for the Cranly of *A Portrait,* was the same size and weight as the Leopold Bloom of *Ulysses,* but little else in Bloom's characterization is based on Byrne. In 1909 Byrne was in his twenties and quite athletic. Leopold Bloom, by contrast, was a middle-aged man of no unusual agility.

After Stephen Dedalus has visited awhile with Bloom that night—it is 2:30 a.m. before Stephen leaves—the contents of Bloom's library are inventoried. Among them is "*Physical Strength and How to Obtain It*, by Eugene Sandow (red cloth)" (709). Elsewhere in *Ulysses* the Sandow exercises for muscular development are twice mentioned. Bloom had been taking them, and thinks to himself that he must resume them. In a locked drawer is a chart of measurements "compiled before, during, and after 2 months of consecutive use of Sandow-Whiteley's pulley-exerciser," indicating that during that period Bloom had increased his chest dimensions from 28 to 29 1/2 inches, his biceps from 9 to 10 inches, and his forearm from 8 1/2 to 9 inches (721).

Such is the way that Joyce's imagination worked. We may assume that, given the story Joyce was telling, it was in order to point up Leopold Bloom's marital problem that Joyce wanted to have him arrive home without his front-door key and be forced to scale the fence in order to let himself into the house. To regain access to his home and his marriage Bloom must resort to extraordinary means. Joyce had designated No. 7 Eccles Street as Bloom's place of residence. In order, therefore, to make it thoroughly plausible that Leopold Bloom could lift himself over that particular iron fence and jump down into the yard, he worked in the business with the Sandow exercises, so that the muscularity of Bloom's upper torso, biceps, and forearms would be appropriate to the deed. This, I believe, is how the item about the exercises made its way into *Ulysses*.

The material itself is factual, in that there was just such a book of exercises, written by such a man, which people in Dublin and elsewhere could purchase and follow. So, too, the iron fence was at last report still there at No. 7 Eccles Street in Dublin for inspection by visiting Joyceans each year on Bloomsday. The larger issue is, Why was this sort of thing so important to James Joyce? What did it have to do with the nature of his imagination?

For, after all, *Ulysses* is a work of fiction: a novel. Leopold Bloom is an invented character. There may be aspects of his personality and his history taken from "real life"—Joyce's, his father's, that of his friend Ettore Schmitz ("Italo Svevo") in Trieste, and no doubt others as well. Yet essentially Bloom, who he is, what he does, the predicament he faces in terms of his wife, and so on, are not drawn from everyday life, as neither are most of the events set in Dublin on June 16, 1904, and involving the main characters.

So if Joyce wanted his fictional character to scale an iron fence in order to regain access to his home, there was nothing to prevent him from lowering the fence outside No. 7 Eccles Street to fit Bloom's imagined physique or, for that matter, from having Bloom reside somewhere else in the city of Dublin where the fence would be the proper height. Why could not the author who created, out of whole cloth, the meeting of Stephen Dedalus and Leopold Bloom, the entire Cyclops chapter at Barney Kiernan's saloon, Father Conmee's stroll through downtown Dublin, Bloom's advertising career, Gerty McDowell on Sandymount shore, Molly Bloom's girlhood at Gibraltar, and numerous other episodes in this richly inventive novel— why could not this author have altered a fence to suit his fictional needs?

The height of a remembered iron fence would not, for example, have bothered a writer such as William Faulkner, whose fictional imagination was not nearly so grounded in historical or geographical minutiae. Faulkner was not infatuated with the documentary details of a time and place, in the way that Joyce was.* But with Joyce it is not merely a matter of a particular road or street; he must give the house number and have the fence at the height that he remembered it, and even make his protagonist engage in a course of exercises in order to be prepared to elevate himself over that fence when the occasion arises. Although James Joyce's library was filled with city directories, maps, and historical and geographical

---

* Yet Faulkner too liked to set his fiction in specific locales sometimes. Cleanth Brooks and I once found ourselves with time on our hands during one of the Faulkner conferences at the University of Mississippi in Oxford, and we decided to try to follow the route that the Bundren family took in their epic journey to Jefferson in *As I Lay Dying.* Because a bridge over a flooding river is out, they must get there by a roundabout way, via the town of Mottson. We knew approximately where the Bundren place was located in Faulkner's mythical Yoknapatawpha County, and our supposition was that to get to Oxford—that is, Jefferson—they would have had to travel west and then come into Oxford from the south, via the town of Water Valley. Was Water Valley, however, Faulkner's fictional Mottson, through which the Bundrens came and where, in *Light in August,* Joe Christmas was apprehended? We drove into Water Valley. There we saw a large building, with a prominent sign, MOTTS PACKING COMPANY.

studies of Dublin, he still frequently wrote to friends and relatives in Dublin to make sure of his details.

Imagine if you will a man engaged in making not a physical leap across an iron fence but an imaginative leap, as it were, across a void. He is engaged in creating something where nothing exists. He is bent upon imitating, mimicking the act of human life itself; he will create imaginary people doing things, participating in actions, feeling emotions about people and events that never existed. His knowledge of those imagined people and their emotions is drawn, of course, from his own experience of people and events, but his objective is not to report with documentary accuracy upon people who already exist, including himself, or events that have already taken place.

Instead he is creating his own imaginary human beings in language, and what they do and say, think and feel, is answerable finally not to history or geography, whether personal or social, but to their own needs as fictional characters. The validity of their behavior, our belief in their plausibility, is to depend not on how specific biographical Dublin residents, whether personally known to us or read about in a book, comported themselves upon actual occasions, but on whether their imagined conduct seems believable and plausible in accordance with what kind of fictional people Joyce has made them into.

Such an act of creativity is a risky thing to attempt. By contrast the author of a work of history or biography, or even of a memoir, does not have to be concerned with that kind of plausibility: his challenges lie elsewhere. If something actually happened, all that it is necessary to point out is *that* it did, and if it was of any importance to indicate its significance.

To select an instance from a very different realm of experience from James Joyce's novel, if we are reading an account of America's entry into World War II, we do not ask whether it is plausible or believable that a full eight hours after the sneak Japanese attack on Pearl Harbor, the U.S. air force in the Philippine Islands was left arrayed wingtip to wingtip at Clark Field, so that it could be wiped out and the Philippines left virtually defenseless from the air. However improbable, that is what happened, and because it did, no additional authority is needed for the inclusion of the incident in a work of history.

The novelist enjoys no such privilege. Credibility and psychological probability are essential. He can use historical or geographical events to help to set the scene and situation for his story, but not for its important actions. James Joyce does not have to convince us that the Liffey River flows through the city of Dublin, or that on the day before the events of *Ulysses* took place, June 16, 1904, a wooden-hulled excursion boat caught fire in the East River in New York City, killing 1,031 persons, so that the Dublin newspapers on Bloomsday would contain headlines about the disaster. That kind of detail is not vital to the believability of Joyce's story—though he had better not have the Thames River flow through Dublin or the SS *Titanic* strike an iceberg and sink in 1904 rather than 1912.

With other kinds of material, however, plausibility—in Aristotelian terms, the probable impossible—is essential. In order to make Stephen Dedalus into an indifferent swimmer (James Joyce was apparently a good swimmer) and his rival Malachi Mulligan into a strong swimmer who has saved men from drowning (as his prototype Oliver St. John Gogarty did), Joyce must labor to make such attributes believable in terms of the kind of human being each is, what he says and does and thinks. Stephen Dedalus must be the brooding intellectual, Malachi Mulligan the outgoing hustler. Coming upon an illogical act, or self-contradictory behavior, as readers we will do what as readers of a work of history we would not think to do: withdraw our assent, refuse to believe in the characterization, decline to take what happens seriously.

For we read fiction not as being about life, as we do with nonfiction; we read it as if it were life itself. In front of all works of fiction (and drama and poetry as well) are the words *Let's pretend,* and paradoxically the fact that what follows is invented rather than recorded intensifies rather than decreases the demand for reasonableness. The very fact that we know that it is not history, not biography, not a chronicle or a memoir about "real life" that we are reading makes it necessary for the novelist to capture our imagination, and cause us to believe in the life*like*ness of what the characters are engaged in doing and thinking and feeling. He must make it possible for us to participate sympathetically in his characters' emotional life *as though* it were ours.

This is why fiction can provide so intense an experience for its readers. By involving our emotions so directly in what happens at every point along the way, it draws us into the imagined life itself, as though it were happening to us. To a far greater extent than with history or biography, our feelings are enlisted. And this is also why, if ever we sense that our feelings are being manipulated and that the emotional investment is not being earned by the characters and their story, we put down the book with contempt. It is cheap, we say; it is sentimental.

To be able to persuade us to make this kind of emotional investment, it follows that the novelist must be bold indeed. He must take risks, push his imagination beyond what is measurable and quantifiable, thrust his presentation of highly volatile emotional behavior beyond the firm earth of documentation and over the void of unbuttressed feeling.

It is understandable, then, that such a novelist will grasp every opportunity he can to support the weight of the narrative he is engaged in imagining, shoring up the foundations of his fictional creation with whatever solid, which is to say grounded and factually verifiable, underpinnings he can find. He must build in safeguards against skepticism on the reader's part (and, I would add, on his own). If he wishes to have a character lift himself over an iron fence, drop to the ground, and let himself into the house, with the imaginative significance that James Joyce has assigned to Bloom's actions in *Ulysses,* he must so see to the "real-life" documentation that the reader will be willing to accept the story's physical and emotional plausibility.

To reiterate, it is emotional life that he is dealing with, of an intensely volatile kind. Leopold Bloom is returning to his home at No. 7. Eccles Street, and Ulysses is also returning home to Penelope at Ithaca, and the realistic fictional twentieth-century homecoming of Bloom the far-wanderer is meant to be as equally and archetypally epic in its human significance as that of the classical Greek seafarer of the *Odyssey.*

Joyce's art is remarkable for numerous reasons, and not least the complexity of its textured surfaces and the intricacy with which the myriad details are linked. In a sense the method is that of the mosaic (Joyce would have made a pun upon that); but to use that image slights the array of connecting structure underlying the almost Byzantine variety. He raised the art of punning to new heights (and sank it to new depths); in *Ulysses* actions and objects have double meanings, and in *Finnegans Wake* the very language itself assumes a quality of layered reference.

In proportion to the effort that went into writing it and the effort required to read it, *Finnegans Wake* has always seemed to me a colossal squandering of Joyce's talent—although given his personality I do not know what else, having once completed *Ulysses,* he could have written in its stead. The need to pursue multiple references and note the way that things link up was central to Joyce's imagination, for the sheer complexity and multiplicity of experience held immense emotional significance for him.

It was the recourse of early readers of *Ulysses* to describe it as a fictional "slice of life," the virtuoso presentation of a sample segment of life in Dublin, Ireland, on a random day in 1904. At the same time, they could sense that there was more going on within its pages than that, but they were not sure just what. We have had to learn how to read it over the years, to discover, in and through the seemingly discontinuous textured surfaces, the workings of the plot, the intensely human story of how Leopold Bloom, his marriage to Molly threatened, gathers the resolve to restore it; how Molly, perilously close to accepting the breakup, will respond to her husband's initiative ("Ill just give him one more chance . . . make him want me thats the only way," 780–81); how Stephen Dedalus, gifted, frustrated, lonely, unwilling to concede his vulnerability and need, learns to accept his own human limitations, so that he can begin to be the artist who will decipher and write "The Book of Myself."

Doing things in Joyce's particular way, however, was not merely an artistic stratagem aimed at hooking the attention of his readers and gaining their assent. It was equally a psychological need on the part of the author. For Joyce himself had to believe in the authenticity of the story he was telling. The motives of his characters—their wishes, their desires, their thoughts—must stand up to the rigorous demands of credibility that his own intelligence could place upon them. He was intensely aware of their ultimate insubstantiality, their status as pure invention. They must be able to sustain their identity in the face of the most ruthless skepticism he could muster. At the very end of *A Portrait of the Artist as a Young Man* Stephen Dedalus sets out as an artist "to forge within the smithy of my soul the uncreated conscience of my race"; the pun is inescapable. In

Finnegans Wake Shem the Penman is by occupation a forger. Not being God, he must counterfeit life with words.

The farther out Joyce ventured, the more pronounced his departure from the firm soil of factual, verifiable existence, the greater his need for the bolstering documentation. Walking along the beach, Stephen Dedalus imagines himself as a blind man:

> Stephen closed his eyes to hear his boots crush crackling wrack and shells. You are walking through it howsomever. I am, a stride at a time. A very short space of time through very short times of space. Five, six: the *nacheinander.* Exactly: and that is the ineluctable modality of the audible. Open your eyes. No. Jesus! If I fell over a cliff that beetles o'er his base, fell through the *nebeneinander* ineluctable. I am getting on nicely in the dark. My ash sword hangs at my side. Tap with it: they do. My two feet in his boots are at the end of his legs, *nebeneinander.* Sounds solid: made by the mallet of *Los Demiurgos.* Am I walking into eternity along Sandymount strand? Crush, crack, crick, crick. (*Ulysses,* 37)

Time—the *nacheinander*—and space—the *nebeneinander*—are real, ineluctable, for this apprentice artist who is not yet a creator, and who is himself a fictional character, a construct of words, a forgery set upon the printed page by his human creator to resemble biological and psychological existence.

We believe in the existence and the importance of Stephen Dedalus and of Leopold and Molly Bloom as imagined human beings because James Joyce has made them so remarkably and convincingly plausible that we can live imaginatively with and through them. A good novel offers us *new emotional experience.* (It is for precisely this reason, I believe, that as we grow older so many of us find ourselves increasingly reluctant to read new fiction. We have already been treated to a generous supply of emotional experience over the years, and have become very choosy about which new varieties we will voluntarily accept. Nonfiction makes no such sustained emotional demand.)

There can be occasions when the people and events being chronicled by a novelist may for one reason or another lie so close to a particular reader's experience that the kind of sympathetic identification necessary to fiction cannot take place. Indeed, in such an instance, being encouraged to involve oneself emotionally in the story through the techniques of the novelist rather than those of the historian might well have quite the opposite result.

For an example of this, one need only read J. F. Byrne's comments, in *Silent Years,* on Joyce's depiction of Bloom going over the front fence at No. 7 Eccles Street to let Stephen Dedalus in through the front door, or Byrne's reaction to the handling of Stephen's conversation with the dean of studies about lighting fires and lamps in *A Portrait of the Artist as a Young Man.* The latter episode, Byrne insists, happened to him, not to the young James Joyce, and there is the sense that he resents Joyce's having appropriated the story for his own purposes.

An "autobiographical" novelist Joyce was, and Stephen Dedalus was essentially modeled upon his youthful self, but he was engaged in creating imagined human beings named Leopold Bloom and Stephen Dedalus, not in re-creating factually accurate descriptions in language of flesh-and-blood people named Byrne and Father Joseph Darlington—or even named James Joyce. Byrne couldn't read it that way. As far as he was concerned, that was not how it really happened.

Yet unless, like Byrne, one is too closely involved in the real-life source to be able to take part in the imaginative transaction, a reader of reasonable sophistication and intelligence, setting in to read *Ulysses* or *A Portrait of the Artist as a Young Man,* cannot remain in doubt for very long that what is unfolding on the printed pages is fiction, not nonfiction. What that reader needs to feel, however, is that what is taking place *could* plausibly have taken place. *If* there were a middle-aged man named Bloom, and he wished to get inside his house to let a younger man named Stephen Dedalus visit him, but had left the front-door key in another pair of trousers, this is how he could and would have vaulted an iron fence to enter via the basement door.

Obviously the ways in which novelists can create lifelike fictional characters and lifelike fictional situations so as to gain our emotional assent are numerous. But in a very real sense, all good fiction is shaped to secure our participation in Leopold Bloom's prodigious leap.

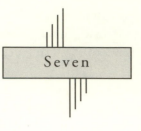

Seven

WHAT ARE ALL THOSE WRITERS
DOING ON CAMPUS?

The question, lords and ladies, is whether teaching Creative Writing is or is not a Good Thing. It has been going on for a half century and more and is accepted as part of the curriculum of almost all American colleges and universities. Yet there are those who continue to disapprove of it.

By Creative Writing I refer to those academic courses, seminars, workshops, tutorials, or whatever that take for their rationale the creation of poems, works of fiction, plays, television scripts—that is, "imaginative" writing.* This is not to say that the imagination is not involved in other forms of writing such as scholarly articles, critical essays, works of history, journalism, and so on. Nor do I wish to get involved in a dispute, whether philosophical, psychological, metaphysical, or pedagogical, over what the term *creative* can or should signify. In practice almost everyone who has been associated with a college or university knows what the words *Creative Writing* mean. They go together; they constitute an entity, which is why I capitalize them. The point at issue is whether the entity is worth bothering with and, if so, why, and for whom.

---

* I know very little about drama, and nothing whatever about film or television scriptwriting, so what follows will have to do solely with the teaching and writing of fiction and poetry. It might be recalled, however, that playwriting groups such as George Pierce Baker's 47 Workshops at Yale and Harvard were among the earliest and best-known writing programs.

The study of Creative Writing is a quite recent development. When Samuel Johnson remarked of the poets of Pembroke College, Oxford, that "Sir, we are a nest of singing birds," he was certainly not referring to what he and certain of his fellow alumni did as part of their academic training. Nobody in Johnson's day or for long years afterward would remotely have contemplated such a development. It is essentially an American academic activity, of relatively recent vintage.

Half a century ago, as a graduate student, I heard a visiting Oxford scholar inform an American audience that "Oxford has never interfered with her poets"—meaning that except for a few extracurricular prize competitions, what young Oxonians might undertake as poets was none of that university's academic concern. He said it with undisguised pride, as if assuring those in attendance that, however imperiled elsewhere, the well of English undefiled was still being preserved safely back at headquarters.

The attitude he was expressing was fully shared by his hosts, the English Department at the Johns Hopkins University in Baltimore, whose faculty and students he was addressing, together with interlopers such as myself. Not only was there no instruction in Creative Writing offered in that department, but works of modern literature were not deemed appropriate for academic investigation beyond the undergraduate level. The prohibition covered anything written after about the year 1910, which is to say, anything later than Henry James.

It was because of this ban, and the attitude toward literary study that it reflected, that there also existed on the Johns Hopkins campus a newly established academic department, the present-day Writing Seminars, offering both an undergraduate major and a master of arts program in creative writing, contemporary literature, and literary criticism.

In those years the campus was crowded with returning World War II veterans who wished to get on with their education. They had spent three years and more in uniform, doing work that most of them would have preferred not to be doing, in places where they would not have chosen to do it. Now they were civilians again and back in school, with the cost of their education covered by the U.S. government. If advanced literary study was what they had in mind, not a few of them were indisposed to observe any such arbitrary chronological distinction. Some even wished to try writing their own fiction and poetry, and not as a spare-time activity between more important matters but as part of their graduate education, while also reading and thinking about the writings of and about James Joyce, W. B. Yeats, T. S. Eliot, Ernest Hemingway, and other authors who wrote in roughly the idiom of their own day. Was there likely ever to be a better time for them to have a try at writing poetry and fiction?

That was why I was there. After being discharged from the Army in 1946, I had finished my senior year of college, then begun work as a newspaper reporter. Meanwhile I had heard that there were university graduate programs in which one could actually be taught how to write novels. The idea came to me to take a year off, enroll at such a university, learn how to write fiction while also getting a great deal of reading done, and then return to newspaper work and write novels in my off-hours. It would be, I thought, as simple as that. So in September of 1948, at age twenty-four, I became a graduate student in the Johns Hopkins Department of Writing, Speech and Drama—long since renamed the Writing Seminars.

I did not learn how to write a novel that year. Instead I stayed on to teach, and when I left six years later it was with an interdepartmental doctorate (*not* in English literature) and a lifelong vocation as a teacher. Over the succeeding five decades I did publish three novels, but mainly mine have been books of nonfiction. I will say, however, that my own students have published dozens of novels and collections of poems and many more books of nonfiction, and are still very much at it. There is a saying that comes to mind, having to do with Those Who Teach.

Still, in order to teach Creative Writing, a talent for writing fiction or poetry of one's own is by no means a requirement. In terms of turning out professional authors it would be difficult, for example, to surpass the record of the late William Blackburn, a specialist in Elizabethan literature who published no fiction or verse of his own that I know of, but whose undergraduate students at Duke University included William Styron, Mac Hyman, Reynolds Price, Fred Chappell, Anne Tyler, and James Applewhite.

Whatever the qualities that make for a satisfactory teacher of Creative Writing, they are not so specialized that someone with intelligence, imagination, a taste for using language, and a sense of what literary works are about cannot handle the job. An effective writing teacher has got to *want* his students to write well, and to be able to communicate his interest in

their doing so. It has always seemed to me that while the study of literature is a broad enough calling, with room for a sufficiently varied array of
approaches, an indispensable requirement for anyone who professes to
teach it is the urge to spread the gospel—to encourage others to discover
and enjoy the uses of the literary imagination. No matter how able a practitioner one is of the art of fiction or poetry, if he has no wish to let others
in on the fun, he has no place teaching it. Conversely, a Creative Writing
teacher need not himself be a *writer,* provided that he is a good *reader* and
wants to show others how a story or poem is put together. The intricacies
of technique are only part of it.

A college or university literature program, it seems to me, that approaches
its curriculum in historical and philological terms alone, and so has no
place for contemporary literature and Creative Writing, is in imminent
peril of pedantry, for by shutting off literary study from the milieu in
which those who take part live and think and feel, whether as teachers or
as students, the outcome is bound to be a species of antiquarianism. It
also works the other way around: the notion that the writing and reading
of stories and poems can be undertaken as a species of vocational education, cut off from awareness of the past, is a prime recipe for superficiality
and the production of froth.

It follows that the idea that only active practitioners of poetry and
fiction can teach Creative Writing is fully as cliquish and snobbish as the
belief that trained scholars alone can teach the reading of literature. In a
field of academic study that needs all the enrichment and imagination it
can get, both are impoverishing attitudes.

It can be gratifying for a writing teacher to know that certain of one's
students have gained distinction as professional authors. That, however, is
scarcely the principal justification for offering classes in Creative Writing.
If it were, then one would have to say that such classes and programs are
not a notably efficient undertaking.

Consider the mathematics alone. According to a recent edition of the
World Almanac, there are approximately fourteen hundred degree-granting
four-year colleges and universities in the United States, not including
community colleges, junior colleges, technical institutes, and the like. It
seems likely that nowadays at least half of those institutions offer one or

more Creative Writing courses and seminars. If we estimate an average enrollment of a dozen students per course, and we hypothesize that in each group several of those so enrolled entertain hopes of becoming professional novelists and/or poets and achieving fame and fortune therefrom, then what are the numerical odds against such hopes being fulfilled? I should think that anyone teaching Creative Writing who adopts that as the measurement of success or failure would be tempted to give it up and try taxi driving or business administration.

Such, however, is *not* where the principal value of Creative Writing courses and programs lies, as if these were no more than vocational education: "earn money in your spare time from writing." A more relevant query would be: What might a young person of reasonable intelligence, imagination, and sensitivity to language have to gain from participating in a college course or program in which he or she will be expected to write poems and stories? And would that gain be more readily obtainable through enrollment in other kinds of courses and programs?

In a seminar we were teaching together, Howard Nemerov once remarked to the students that "we're in the wisdom business," by which he meant that to write poems and fiction was to seek to get at meanings, not as abstract ideas or impersonal description but in terms of what we feel. To write a poem or a story is to attempt to re-create emotional life in words, whether directly or indirectly it does not matter. The key word is *re-create.* In order to do that, one must be able to identify and objectify one's experience, not merely undergo it—which is no simple matter. Having felt deeply is not enough; the experience of doing so must be reenacted in words. Creative Writing is a form of knowledge—self-knowledge.

Surely the shaping of ideas and emotions into stories and poems— and, one might add, the reverse procedure as well—can only enrich one's own perceptions. In the same way that, for example, a skilled musician's awareness of technique enables him to grasp *how* a composer's imagination achieves its melodic impact, so the imaginative insights of a literary composition can be made more fully available through the experience of having sought to use language for similar ends. It is for this reason that I am strongly in favor of encouraging poets and novelists to teach literature as well as Creative Writing courses.

I think of the young men and women who were graduate students in the Johns Hopkins Writing Seminars some fifty-odd years ago. Of those whose subsequent careers I know about, one became a well-known novelist, two others published several novels apiece, three published poetry extensively and several others occasionally, and one published some short fiction. All of them also taught Creative Writing. Five others went on to earn doctorates (not in the Johns Hopkins English Department) and teach literature. Another became a nationally syndicated newspaper columnist. Two became dramatic arts teachers and directors; another taught film history and production. One wrote and produced advertising; one entered book publishing. Three that I know of became ministers. What the others ended up doing I cannot say, but there is no reason to believe that their subsequent careers were not reasonably fulfilling.

All these were graduate students, enrolled in a master of arts program. For undergraduate students, there would doubtless be a wider dispersion of postacademic careers. From what they studied in their courses and seminars, some drew more directly than others. The point is that while very few of the students enrolled in a given Creative Writing program will probably earn their living by writing fiction or poetry, most are likely to make both personal and professional use of the aptitudes, interests, and insights that as apprentice writers they sought to develop in classes and seminars. I believe that overall the ratio of light to heat will compare favorably with that of any other program of study.

Can Creative Writing be taught? Obviously imagination is an essential ingredient in writing poetry and fiction, and no one can teach imagination to another who is without it. Moreover, imagination is God-given, or in any event DNA-provided. The question thus becomes, If they come equipped with an adequate supply of imagination, can students be taught how to use it to create poetry and fiction? On the assumption that the answer to that is *Yes,* what a class or program in Creative Writing does is to try to facilitate that process.

Presumably the students enrolled in a course specifically devoted to the writing of poetry or fiction will have demonstrated both an interest in doing so and at least a degree of aptitude for it. The process will almost certainly require both some learning and, especially at the outset, some *un*-learning.

In the early 1960s, at Hollins College, we began conducting an annual poetry contest, in which high school English teachers were encouraged to submit groups of poems by their students, with our own students evaluating and choosing the winners. What we found each year was that if in a given school's batch of entries the first couple of poems that were read showed an interesting use of language and freshness of attitude, then the chances were good that all of the poems submitted from that school would merit attention. If, on the other hand, the first several poems encountered were repetitious in form and loaded with conventional poetic clichés, the likelihood was that the other poems from that school, no matter how many were being submitted, would exhibit the same flatness of diction and idea.

What this meant was not that the students in one high school were more imaginatively gifted than those at the other. Rather, it indicated that the students at one school were being exposed to poetry written in the idiom of their own time, and were learning how to use language to explore their experience, while those at another school had been taught that to write a poem meant to set down rhymed abstractions in capital-P Poetic diction. If the latter students were to develop their ability to write verse, they would have to learn to put aside certain received assumptions about what a poem was and was not, assumptions that were crippling their efforts to re-create what they thought and felt in poems. That was some four decades ago and more, and presumably the styles have changed some since then, but the need for clearing away stereotyped poetic responses and facile approximations remains.

One way to further that objective—I think by far the most important way—is to introduce the student to writing that *can* speak with greater immediacy to the student's needs and interests, in language that will image these with acceptable authenticity and vividness. A teacher can help to make it possible for that to happen. Especially on the beginning level, apprentice poets and fiction writers need to read what their contemporaries have written. By contemporaries I mean authors who have written with something of the same language conventions and idiom as theirs, and whose everyday life has been confronted in terms that are reasonably recognizable.

Anyone who has dealt with college-age students is familiar with the way in which a young person can be "turned on" by the discovery of a particular writer. I think of the intensity with which several talented students of my own, now in their fifties and sixties, responded, in their late teens and early twenties, to such writers as J. D. Salinger and Carson McCullers. (A generation earlier it might have been Thomas Wolfe.) As often as not it will be by introducing students to a literary milieu, enabling young would-be writers to come upon an author who seems to speak directly to them, that a teacher can help to stimulate the kind of relationship that Herman Melville once described as the "shock of recognition." Melville meant the discovery by one writer that another, usually older, writer has been addressing the kind of interests and concerns that until then the discoverer had believed to be too subjective to be shared and expressed. Walt Whitman expressed this as well as anybody when he remarked, "I was simmering, simmering, until Emerson brought me to a boil."

It has been objected that young writers will be better off if allowed to make these discoveries for themselves; supposedly such transactions are more meaningful when negotiated entirely on their own. This seems dubious to me. In the first place, the most that one can ever do is to expose the young writer to the work of other writers. Presumably the teacher, by virtue both of having done more reading than the student and of having identified where the student's own interests lie, can suggest that this or that writer might be especially useful for the student to read. The response, if any, to the author thus suggested will depend on the young writer. You can lead a horse to water, etc.

As for any imagined discouragement of originality that may be involved, it ought to be obvious that all young writers must go through stages in which their work will be influenced by certain other writers. This is a necessary development. Whatever may be true for other art forms such as music, in the writing of poetry or fiction there are no child prodigies, no Mozarts or Yehudi Menuhins. The ability to articulate one's thoughts and emotions in language can be nurtured only through extensive—and intensive—reading and adaptation. Technique is only the vehicle for a complex creative transaction. This is not to say, of course, that potential talent cannot be recognized early on, only that it will be just that: *promising;* an augury of future achievement, which may or may not be realized.

In the course of trying on this or that way of saying things in language, the apprentice writer learns to come closer not only to fulfilling the demands of his own creative urge but also to recognizing what those demands really are. In other words, to create is to discover, and to read what another author has written can help a young writer to get at his own experience. Whether that young writer will prove able to make use of what he finds out is another matter.

It is also quite true that the example of a new, alluring style can be so overwhelming that a young writer may be swamped by the discovery—as many an echoing of *Look Homeward, Angel,* including mine, once indicated. Yet no two writers will have exactly the same needs, whether of style or content, and it seems quite unlikely that a young writer with anything important to say will remain under the lasting domination of another's approach, however attractive it might seem upon first encounter.

Anyone who has taught beginning writers knows that one of the principal jobs can be helping them to recognize what they are actually writing about, as distinguished from what they may think it is. A hypothetical example: the student writer sets out, let us say, to tell about a youth taking part in and losing a sailboat race, with the suspense centered upon who will cross the finish line first. In terms of the way that the youth's character and personality have been developed, his attitude toward narrowly losing the sailboat race seems overwrought and out of proportion to the occasion. In the course of narrating the story, there is a brief, seemingly casual mention of an earlier disagreement between the youth who is sailing the boat and his father.

One's first reaction upon reading the story would probably be that the excessive reaction to losing the race should be toned down. When discussing the story with the student and noting the imbalance, however, the teacher comes to suspect that the father-son disagreement is of considerably more importance to what the original experience signified to the young author than the story as written would have it.

What happened was that the young writer's conscious intentions and his creative imagination were functioning on separate frequencies. He had set out to tell about sailboat racing. His imagination had picked up the fact that the relationship with the father figured in what sailing and losing the race signified to the young author, even though in thinking about the sailboat race as a story he had not intended to get into that. If the story is to move beyond describing what happens in a sailboat race itself and into what the experience means emotionally for the protagonist—which is to say, if it is to work *as fiction*—both themes must be adequately developed in the telling. Any chance that the student writer has of advancing past the beginning level of fiction-writing will depend upon an aptitude for doing just that.

In terms of the uses of courses in Creative Writing, one may object that any young person with the necessary talent and desire to write fiction must inevitably figure out such connections and relationships on his own, and for the teacher to do that for him will stifle his own initiative. As well insist that an art instructor who shows a beginning class in painting how to handle chiaroscuro is unduly influencing the students. Surely what matters is what the apprentice then does, whether with paintbrush and oils or, for the young writer, with words.

By no means least among the potential uses of Creative Writing courses is the fact that a group situation is involved. On the obvious level this means that the student participants have a ready-made audience to serve as a sounding board for trying out their writings. By its very nature the creation of fiction and poetry is a solitary activity, composed in private and designed ultimately to be judged as words printed in ink on paper, with no author present to provide vocal modulations and emphases or to answer questions about what the writer intended. Typically the beginning writer is uncertain of his own efforts and eager to know whether the words he is setting down will convey the meaning he wishes to communicate. The comments and encouragement of a group of one's peers, basically in sympathy with what one is engaged in doing while also aware that uncritical praise will serve no purpose, can be quite useful.

To take proper advantage of such an opportunity, the would-be writer must be able to use criticism without being threatened by it. If what the student is looking for is not comment but adulation, and if he is so without confidence in his own worth that he cannot tolerate the slightest intimation that a story or poem could stand emendation and improvement, then participation in a Creative Writing program is contraindicated, as the MDs say.

What I have told those who read the draft of a story to a student group is that when there is query and criticism, the chances are that something is missing in the story that should be there. Because the story itself is not controlling the terms on which it is being encountered, the auditors are attempting to fill in the gap. The proposed suggestions may not be in themselves appropriate or relevant, but they should be seen as an indication that what has been written thus far may not have been made sufficiently clear.

Whenever I hold forth on the virtues and vices of Creative Writing courses, I confront the comments of a gifted friend, dead now these forty years, who was considerably less convinced of their worth. Flannery O'Connor took a master of arts degree in the University of Iowa Writers Workshop, which very fact is of itself a powerful recommendation for Creative Writing programs, but later she wrote that she didn't believe in classes where students criticize each other's manuscripts. "Such criticism," she wrote, "is generally composed in equal parts of ignorance, flattery, and spite. It's the blind leading the blind, and it can be dangerous."*

My own experience with teaching writing students and working with authors makes me believe that Flannery, who always took a skeptical view of anything that smacked of secular betterment or educational and social innovation, very much overstated her case. I have seen too many young writers benefit from just such sessions, at a time when the encouragement

---

* This and the two quotations by Flannery O'Connor cited below are taken from "The Nature and Aim of Fiction," in her spritely collection of writings, *Mystery and Manners: Occasional Prose,* selected and edited by Sally and Robert Fitzgerald (New York: Farrar, Straus and Giroux, 1969), 86, 84, 86, in that order. It should be pointed out that, as the editors explain in their introduction, "The Nature and Aim of Fiction" was pieced together by them from typescripts of an assortment of talks delivered on various occasions.

of knowing that what they were writing was being taken seriously by their contemporaries was very welcome indeed.

There is even something to be said for the sense of competitiveness that can come from being involved in a student group (or any other kind of group). One need not be a Norman Mailer, or an Ernest Hemingway envisioning oneself as whipping de Maupassant and fighting two draws with Stendhal, in order to profit from the wish to keep pace with or outdo a fellow author. Whatever may have been Flannery's experience, my own has been that while students may vie among themselves, they are at the same time generally supportive of each other's efforts. That good writers so often seem to arrive on the literary scene in bunches is evidence enough that, especially when young, they can have much to gain from that kind of association. I have noticed that the writers of a student group tend to stay in close touch with each other long after graduation, however widely their work and paths may then diverge.

In any event, a potential writer who can be so readily led astray by classroom commentary, whether *pro* or *con,* is unlikely to be able to stand the gaff for very long, once out in the cold cruel world. Certainly I can't imagine Flannery herself ever allowing such comment to deflect her from her chosen art.

Flannery also wrote, "Everywhere I go I'm asked if I think the universities stifle writers. My opinion is that they don't stifle enough of them. There's many a best-seller that could have been prevented by a good teacher." I tend to take the same view of popular fiction, but whatever the crimes, heinous and otherwise, of Creative Writing programs, very few who teach in them are engaged in encouraging the kind of writing that produces best-sellers. The customary complaint runs, if anything, just the other way; allegedly the participants in writing programs in the ivied towers of colleges and universities are deprived of the necessary embroilment in Real American Life that could give them access to the larger reading public.

The Creative-Writing-as-Hothouse-Plant hypothesis is double-edged: (1) Writers don't belong in universities because they lack contact with the daily rat race and are encouraged to write for the educated elite instead of the common reader. (2) Creative Writing programs encourage far too many moderately talented young people to seek careers as authors, thereby augmenting the mediocrity available to readers and setting up a kind of literary Gresham's Law whereby an oversupply of routine competence drowns out what is exceptional and superior. To quote Flannery O'Connor again, "so many people can now write competent stories that the short story as a medium is in danger of dying of competence. We want competence, but competence by itself is deadly. What is needed is the vision to go with it, and you do not get this from a writing class."

Neither can it be got from a newsroom, a trout stream, a theological seminary, a police station, a boiler factory, or a writers' conference. Artistic vision—or, to forgo the religious implications, which however Flannery certainly intended, artistic *imagination*—is what the student writer has to contribute on his own, and, as noted earlier, it is not anything that can be taught, whether in a writing class or anywhere else. Still, before we get to separating literary sheep from goats too readily, we might remember that not everyone who possesses the requisite artistic vision learns how to deploy it at the same pace. Marcel Proust and Walker Percy were in their forties when their first novels appeared.

The claim that Creative Writing has made the vitality go out of our literature has been advanced on various sides and for various reasons. For all I know it may be so, but given so many previous pronouncements to that effect, dating back to long before the invention of Creative Writing programs and writers in residence, I am skeptical. In truth there have often been times when literature seems at low ebb to those surveying the cultural horizon. In part the evaluation depends on who is making the measurements, and what is held to constitute low, high, and slack water.

Recently, in the 1970s, not only was the novel as an art form pronounced dead, having been succeeded by the "nonfiction novel," but the literary subgenre in which Flannery O'Connor had excelled, Southern fiction, after flowering from the 1920s through the 1950s, was widely declared to be withering in the verbena patch. Yet in the 1980s, when Shannon Ravenel and I founded a small trade publishing house, Algonquin Books, within five years' time we turned up first novels by Clyde Edgerton, Kaye Gibbons, Jill McCorkle, Larry Brown, and Lewis Nordan—three North Carolinians and two Mississippians. As for the "nonfiction novel," that turned out to be little more than a promotional device for Truman Capote.

There used to be a press agent in Baltimore who liked to open a comment with "In my humble opinion," and then add parenthetically, "and I know goddamn well I'm right." For myself, when it comes to the business of blaming college and university Creative Writing programs for anything so complex as the reportedly failing health of the national letters, I feel that way, too. The cart is being placed before the horse, or the tenor before the vehicle, or however the saying goes. *Why are the writers in the universities?* Only in recent years have they taken up residence there *as* writers. And what has happened to make colleges and universities more receptive to poets and novelists? What accounts for the apparently unslaked contemporary demand for Creative Writing programs?

Before the days of Creative Writing, poets and even fiction writers were sometimes members of college and university faculties, but always as scholars in traditional fields of academic study—Longfellow in foreign languages, Henry Adams in history, Housman in classical languages, Stephen Leacock as an economist, and so on. In the 1920s and 1930s there were occasional appointments of writers to teach writing, mainly poetry. Not until Creative Writing programs began to gain in popularity following the close of World War II, however, did the presence of poets and novelists on campus become commonplace, first as writers in residence, then as teachers. These days it is even considered appropriate for them to teach classes in literature as well as writing, on the theory that a practitioner might possibly possess useful insights into the workings of other practitioners' imaginations.

Depending upon the individual author's preferences, the advantage of teaching in a university is that it is a way to earn a living while working with literature and writing, and also that there will be time and energy available for one's own writing. An author might well prefer to do nothing but write, but ordinarily that will require inherited or subsidized wealth. Today as always the number of novelists who can earn their livings from writing literary fiction—the kind of fiction that authors such as Flannery O'Connor, John Updike, Saul Bellow, Eudora Welty, V. S. Naipaul, John Barth, etc., wrote and write—can be counted on the fingers and thumbs of a critic's hands. As for poets supporting themselves and their families from the proceeds of the sale of their verse alone, the very thought is fantastic. Not since Victorian times has writing good poetry paid living wages for the poetry itself, and then only to a very few poets. Today it is strictly a noncommercial, cottage-type activity.

It is true that literary renown produces lecturing and reading fees, but here again, the invitations for these usually arrive from colleges and universities, so that this can scarcely be considered a way to avoid the allegedly enervating cultural airs of the campus. Moreover, such invitations do not precede but follow upon the achievement of recognition for one's writings, while the problem of earning a living must ordinarily be addressed well before that, if indeed the day ever arises.

A longtime friend of mine, Shelby Foote, liked to argue that a writer shouldn't get married, have children, take on a mortgage, or otherwise incur the obligations of unbounded domesticity. Rather, a writer's devotion should be solely to art. Most writers, however, have been unable or unwilling to dispense with such extracurricular activities, and so, unless independently wealthy, must seek gainful employment. So, if not teaching, what then?

The obvious response is, Well, what did they do back before Creative Writing programs were invented? The answer is, depending on the temperament and aptitudes of the individual, whatever came best to hand. For an author who must earn a livelihood other than directly from his literary production, which is to say, for all but a very few authors, there were and are essentially two choices. One way is to work at something as close to one's career and aptitudes as possible. Teaching is an obvious example; so are editing, journalism, script writing, advertising, or whatever one's interests might be. Thus Saul Bellow taught, Ernest Hemingway was a newspaper correspondent and later wrote outdoors articles for *Esquire,* James Dickey wrote advertising copy, William Faulkner and Scott Fitzgerald movie scripts, and so on. The alternative is to seek a routine physical or clerical job, demanding the expenditure of as little as possible of the particular skills and energies that imaginative writing requires. Nathanael West, working as a night clerk in a hotel, Larry Brown as a fireman, and Alex Haley as a U.S. Coast Guardsman are examples of this.

For purposes of writing about it, some kinds of work are probably open to a greater range of immediately usable experience than others.

The more important equation by far, however, is *who* will be having the experience. One could cite examples and multiply entities unnecessarily, but to what purpose it is difficult to say. When I hear all the argumentation about whether novelists and poets ought or ought not to be teaching in universities, I am reminded of a famous World War I cartoon by Bruce Bairnsfather, showing two helmeted British Tommies peering out of a shell hole in no-man's-land, while all about them shrapnel and shard are bursting. "Well, if yer knows of a better hole," one is saying to the other, "go to it."

To return to questions previously raised. Why are the writers in the universities? Because that is where their readership is. (By universities, of course, I mean those who are currently enrolled or teaching there, and a segment of those who have previously done so.) The poets have known this for some time. The fiction writers are now finding it out. The universities and colleges want them there because they in turn have finally begun to realize that if the study of English and American literature is to escape the fate of Greek and Latin, and not become an antiquarian activity, there can be no artificial barrier enforced between the study of historical literature and the study of the fiction and poetry of their own time and place.

Finally, why are the writers teaching Creative Writing? Because they are teaching people how to *read*. It comes down to that. I can't think of a better reason for them to be on campus. If this be elitism, make the most of it.

Eight

THE PROGRESS OF POETRY: OR, A FUNNY THING HAPPENED ON THE WAY TO THE BOOKSTORE

Of composts shall the Muse disdain to sing?
—James Grainger, *The Sugar-Cane*

Poets are having a bifurcating time of it these days. On the one hand the medium itself, as an art form, flourishes. There is probably more poetry being published nowadays than ever before, and the level of competence is quite high, probably higher than it ever was. On the other hand, poetry has no general audience, not even a general literary audience. There is no center, no acknowledged forum, whether geographical or commercial, where the leading practitioners can be identified and their productions sorted and graded.

New York City and Boston used to perform this function, however unevenly, with periodical help from Chicago. No more. Except for a very few token poets, the metropolitan trade publishing houses—which once brought out the new books of verse and saw to it that critics reviewed them, bookstores stocked them, and the general reading public recognized their names—have given it up. These days new poetry is published by university presses, small presses, in chapbooks, "little" magazines, literary quarterlies, broadsides—but very seldom commercially.

It would be convenient to be able to blame it all on television, which certainly hasn't helped matters so far as encouraging people to read is concerned, but it was happening before television became—to coin a phrase—part of the picture. What the advent of TV did was to confirm and accelerate the process. The book publishing business was converted into a branch of the entertainment industry, and this in turn had the result of bringing down the auspices under which poetry was published commercially.

In point of fact, poetry rarely has done much more than break even financially, in any event not since the days of the Good Gray Poets. What got new verse published commercially in ancient times—that is, before the arrival of commercial television—was the presence of the gentlemanly aura that used to permeate the book trade. Publishing was held to be something of a socially select operation, like classical music and yacht racing. As often as not the leading houses were owned by individuals or families, who believed it appropriate to their cultural and social image to bring out collections of new verse, even if the chances of earning back production costs were only fair to middling. This was all right, because printing and binding were reasonably cheap, editorial and clerical salaries were quite low, and other books of a less exalted nature could be counted upon to take up the slack. The investment houses on Wall Street weren't interested in anything that was conducted so casually and that produced so little revenue per dollar expended. So in those days poetry still counted for something. Each year when the Pulitzer Prize for poetry was announced, the proud publisher of the winning collection rushed out a new printing, with a band around the jacket proclaiming its canonization.

In the years after World War II this began changing, and rapidly. Television, which encouraged the star system and the blockbuster novel, set the pace; the book clubs and the "paperback revolution" drastically altered the economics of the industry; and the financial slump of the 1970s finished off not a few once-proud literary imprints. Book publishing was assimilated into the Age of the Conglomerates. The corporate executives who now controlled the selection and marketing of new books were not impressed by literary renown as such. The cultural and social distinction that a trade publishing house commanded from having well-known poets in its stable was held to be no longer worth the money and time involved.

The result is that publishing poetry has become in effect a cottage industry. Small presses, which in actuality if not in intent are mostly nonprofit, and university presses, which are subsidized and not expected to make money, took over the job. They have done it well, and with appropriate enthusiasm. Meanwhile the poets have moved on campus, where their audience mainly is, and where they earn most of their reading fees.

At the same time, such nationwide and transatlantic renown as a T. S. Eliot, a Robert Frost, or a W. H. Auden once enjoyed among a general literary audience seems possible no more. Who won the Pulitzer and Bollingen Prizes for poetry last year? The year before? What are the odds against a new collection of poems receiving critical notice in the *New York Times Book Review* or the *Washington Post Book World* today? I can think of a half-dozen good poets, each of whom has published at least six books and more, and whose work is admired by coteries of discriminating readers, yet who command little or no general literary reputation. If the average reader of new books were asked who any of them were or what they wrote, unless they were located within the particular geographical area of the reader's residence their names would signify nothing. 'Taint fair! But 'tis true.

As for what accounts for this attenuation of reader interest in contemporary poetry, I think that most general readers would declare that poetry is "too hard to read." By this would be meant that the intensification of language that good poetry necessarily entails requires an intellectual concentration beyond that of prose, so that the demand made upon the reader is greater. The very fact that the basic unit of poetry is the line, not the sentence, and this whether rhymed or not, serves to interrupt the advance of the thought being expressed, and directs attention instead to the images and the individual properties of words and phrases. These are made to work both with and against each other, to contrast as well as to confirm. All this takes considerably more time per line and page to comprehend, and involves sustained cerebration, so that it should be no surprise that ordinary readers resist the outlay of effort. In short, poetry has traveled a long distance away from "The Building of the Ship" and "Crossing the Bar."

In order for poetry to have arrived at its present condition, a lengthy evolutionary process has had to take place, and it is this that I want to trace.

By definition, the writing and reading of poetry have always been, and continue to be, elitist operations. They presuppose the possession and use of literacy and leisure. Until several hundred years ago, the primary possessors of both these articles were the propertied well-to-do and the clergy. The rise of an urban middle class had the effect of expanding the ranks of the educated, so that membership in the cultural and intellectual elite was no longer confined to the socially accredited and the ministry. It remained, however, a select group; what was made less restrictive were the membership requirements.

The expansion of the reading public was concurrent with the vogue of Neoclassicism, which among other things was a way of refining manners, stylizing taste, and regularizing culture. More than mere happenstance, too, was the simultaneous development of the novel, which opened up middle-class attitudes to literary use and made possible the more accurate documentation of everyday experience in literature.

The response of the poets of the eighteenth century to these developments is interesting. There was a general move toward stylized diction and poetic language, aimed at intensifying verse through heightening it to the status of epigram. The result was to place a premium upon wit and to formalize the movement of thought into rhymed couplets. The leading poets of the period—Pope, Swift, Johnson—were not lyricists so much as moralists and ironists.

At the same time, the hereditary prestige of poetry was such that attempts were made to open up its civic boundaries to subject matter, and ways of handling it, that had previously been reserved for prose. Poems had been used by the Elizabethans and Jacobeans primarily to voice upper-stratum concerns such as love, martial valor, and pastoral celebration. Now not only was the High Style, previously reserved for the well-born, adapted to middle-class experience, but vulgar objects as well were to be gilded by more poetic euphemisms.

The clash of social modes, intentional or otherwise, has always been a prime vehicle for humor, and the circumlocutions that certain poets of the age employed to poeticize what was otherwise held to be too-mundane subject matter are always good for a laugh, as when Lord Hervey of Ickworth asks,

Would any feather'd maiden of the wood,
Or scaly female of the peopled flood,
When lust and hunger call'd, its force resist?
　　("Epistle to Mr. Fox, from Hampden Court")

By using embroidered, anthromorphic imagery to avoid having to say birds and fish, he is engaged in poeticizing his experience. The eighteenth and early nineteenth centuries were a heyday for such writing, for poetry was thought of in terms of an elevating, uplifting art, more "literary" and more ennobling than prose. The widespread expansion of literacy was producing numerous ambitious poets who now possessed the means to publish their poetic effusions. Sometimes, in works such as Dyer's *The Fleece* and Grainger's *The Sugar-Cane,* the long poem was attempted for purposes of descriptive documentation that the prose novel, with its capacity for cataloging the details of everyday social and commercial experience, could more comfortably accommodate.

　　The Stuffed Owl: An Anthology of Bad Verse, edited by D. B. Wyndham Lewis and Charles Lee (1930), offers page after page of excerpts from such poetry. Here, for example, are lines from James Grainger's *The Sugar-Cane* (1759):

Of composts shall the Muse disdain to sing?
Nor soil her heavenly plumes? The sacred Muse
Nought sordid deems, but what is base; nought fair,
Unless true Virtue stamp it with her seal.
Then, planter, wouldst thou double thine estate,
Never, ah! never, be asham'd to tread
Thy dung-heaps.

　　The sacred Muse belongs to the poetic High Style; composts and dung heaps do not, and neither does the kind of sensibility that would consciously set out to make them acceptable to the High Style, instead of the other way around. But that is what the poet was intent on doing, as in these lines from "The Temple of Nature," by Erasmus Darwin, grandfather of Charles:

So still the Tadpole cleaves the watery vale,
With balanc'd fins and undulating tail;

New lungs and limbs proclaim his second birth,
Breathe the dry air, and bound upon the earth.
Allied to fish, the Lizard cleaves the flood,
With one-cell'd heart, and dark frigescent blood;
Half-reasoning Beavers long-unbreathing dart
Through Eirie's waves with perforated heart;
With gills and lungs respiring Lamphreys steer,
Kiss the rude rocks, and suck till they adhere

Then there is the poet who aspires to the elevated diction and lofty outlook of the high style, but lacks a firm grasp upon the connotative properties of the language he or she makes bold to use, as in these lines allegedly
written—I am skeptical—by "A Housemaid Poet" of the early nineteenth
century:

O Moon, when I gaze on thy beautiful face,
Careering along through the boundaries of space,
The thought has often come into my mind
If I ever shall see thy glorious behind.

It will be recalled that when Wordsworth, in the Preface to the Second
Edition of the *Lyrical Ballads* (1800), declared that his poems were written
in the language of humble and rustic life, Coleridge demurred. Wordsworth's contention was that "such a language, arising out of repeated experience and regular feelings, is a more permanent, and a far more philosophical language, than that which is normally substituted for it by Poets,
who think that they are conferring honour upon themselves and their art,
in proportion as they separate themselves from the sympathies of men." To
which Coleridge responded that "were there excluded from Mr. Wordsworth's poetic compositions all, that a literal adherence to the theory of
his preference would exclude, two-thirds at least of the marked beauties
of his poetry must be erased" (*Biographia Literaria*, 1816).

What Wordsworth did do was to prune from the language of poetry the
elaborate devices—personification, circumlocution, tortured inversion of
word order, public (as opposed to personal) iteration, emphasis upon sing-
song meter, mythological ornamentation, excessive abstraction, addiction
to the rhymed couplet—that stultified eighteenth-century poetry in the

hands of all but its best practitioners. But his own "egotistical sublime," however simpler and more personal, was still very much the High Style:

> Thou, whose exterior semblance doth belie
>   Thy soul's immensity;
> Thou best Philosopher, who yet dost keep
> Thy heritage, thou Eye among the blind,
> That, deaf and silent, read'st the eternal deep,
> Haunted forever by the eternal mind—
>   Mighty Prophet! Seer blest!
>   ("Ode: Intimations of Immortality")

An advantage of the High Style is that it can enable both intensification of emotion and subtlety of expression, which is one reason Aristotle in the *Poetics* assigned its use to Tragedy and relegated the Low Style to Comedy. If there is approximate agreement between poet and audience on what is and is not acceptable literary language and subject matter, then both poet and audience are freed of the repeated need to make decisions about taste and appropriateness. A disadvantage is that the agreement may become too restrictive, forcing the exclusion of too important a portion of the poet's experience, or else, in the poet's efforts to avoid letting it so, may cause excessive circumlocution, euphemism, generalities, abstraction, and stylistic mannerisms.

As with all writing, but particularly with poetry, a potential opposition exists between the wish to chronicle one's experience and the conventions of literary style within which one seeks to do it. The need to accommodate the one to the other—it works both ways—can produce a creative tension that makes for memorable poetry. But the conventions can change over the years, and, as we have seen, one period's High Style can become another's literary straitjacket.

The manner in which poets have striven to handle the problem of adapting their subject matter to the stylistic conventions of their time can be demonstrated in the way that successive translators have acted to render into contemporary socially acceptable English a passage of poetry written in another language. The poet Dante, writing in Italian on the eve of the Renaissance and before the subsequent division of literary language into

High and Low Styles, made use of words and images, and the attitude accompanying them, that in a later era would be thought much too vulgar for inclusion in a work having to do with God's arrangements for human beings after death. Thus in Canto 21 of the *Inferno,* Dante and Virgil visit a ditch of boiling pitch, into which a cadre of devils are engaged in dipping persons who during their lifetimes were guilty of the sale of church offices. The head devil details a squad to escort the two visitors to a bridge over the ditch. At that point the Italian text reads as follows:

> *ma prima avea ciascun la lingua stretta*
> *coi denti, verso lor duca, per cenno;*
> *ed egli avea del cul fatto trombetta.*

Unafraid of mingling the higher style with the lower, Dante is in no way reluctant to use the vulgar word *cul* in a religious poem. Charles S. Singleton's English translation (1970) renders the lines as follows: "but first each pressed his tongue between his lips at their leader for a symbol, and he had made a trumpet of his arse." In other words, the devils signify their assent by a kind of Bronx cheer, and their leader returns the compliment by farting back.

This was all very well, but when later it came to be translated into Neoclassical English there were problems. Once the doctrine of stylistic separation came into use in the later seventeenth century, thereafter for English-language readers it would not do to render the last line of the canto literally. The eighteenth century's way of handling such things, as we have seen, was by paraphrase, typically with a classical or mythological reference. In 1802, when the high Augustan style had not yet been undercut by the *Lyrical Ballads,* the Reverend Henry Boyd, A.M., making use of classical mythology, rendered "*et egli avea del cul fatto trombetta*" as "and loud ÆOLIAN fifes their fury 'suage." A little later, in 1814, another divine, the Reverend H. F. Cary, A.M., opted for inverted word order and left the choice of musical instruments to the individual reader: "which he with sound obscene triumphant gave."

After Wordsworth and the Romantics arrived, however, elaborate figures of speech were no longer in fashion. The most widely read of nineteenth-century poets, Longfellow, translating Dante in 1867, was more direct: "and he had made a trumpet of his rump." In 1891 Charles Eliot Norton repeated him verbatim. The Temple Classics translation of 1900 altered the word order to something closer to the original: "and he of his rump had made a trumpet." In 1894 Arthur John Butler, translating for the Macmillan Company, made only a mild adjustment: "and he had made a trumpet of his rear." As late as 1939 Butler's innovation was repeated word for word by John D. Sinclair for the Oxford University Press.

Yet the poetry of Modernism, with its greater reliance upon the vernacular, was by then taking over. Jefferson Butler Fletcher, also translating for Macmillan in 1931, gave the line as "had made a bugle of his own backside." With World War II came a general broadening of parlance; thus in 1948 Thomas G. Bergin, for the Croft Classics, rendered the line as "emitting from his arse a bugle blast." Dorothy Sayers, also in 1948, was more restrained: "he promptly made a bugle of his breech." The poet John Ciardi, for New American Library in 1954, was matter-of-fact about it: "and he had made a trumpet of his ass."

Then came the *Lady Chatterley's Lover* decision, the Beat bards, and the New Left. Elizabeth Jennings, translating Canto 21 for the BBC's Third Programme in 1966, described what had happened at the ditch of boiling pitch thusly: "Barbiger made a bugle of a fart." Mark Musa, for Indiana University Press in 1971, was more graphic: "and he blew back with his bugle of an ass-hole." C. H. Sisson, for Carcanet New Press, Ltd., in 1980, went back to the more virtuoso musical horn and traditional spelling, but did not flinch from the anatomical detail: "and he sounded a trumpet call from his arse-hole." And Nicholas Kilmer, for Branden Publishing Company in 1985, perhaps after attending a Red Sox game, decided upon something dramatic: "*ed egli avea del cul fatto trombetta*" now became "who, with his asshole, bugled, 'Charge!'"

I have suggested that the High Style of Neoclassical English and French poetry had a social as well as literary role to perform. In the nineteenth-century United States this was very much so. The political ideals of the new nation were those of democratic egalitarianism; there was to be no inherited privilege, no aristocracy. Yet the belles lettres were the traditional fruits of leisure, classical education, and contemplation, which had gone hand in hand with wealth and hereditary status. It seemed important, therefore, to demonstrate that American experience, though middle class and without the usual artistic condiments, was worthy of employment for purposes of literary creativity. As might be expected, such demonstrations tended to take the form of an earnest effort to uplift that experience above the dross and meanness of everyday life, both in language and in subject matter.

Nature and the natural world were considerably more amenable to such purposes than what went on in cities, towns, barnyards, factories, kitchens, railroad stations, theaters, and so on. With the compelling example of the English Romantic poets for a model, the outsetting American bards, male and female both, did their best to adapt the language conventions and philosophical attitudes of Wordsworth, Keats, Shelley, Tennyson, etc., to the woods and templed hills of the still largely undeveloped continent.

The result was a poetic High Style that was notably distanced from everyday discourse. Thus Sarah Hall of Philadelphia describes a river's progression through Pennsylvania and Maryland to union with successively larger bodies of water, and closes with an echo of "Tintern Abbey":

> But silent through the glade retired and wild,
> Between the shaded banks on either hand,
> Till circling yonder mead—he yields his name,
> Nor proudly, Susquehanna! boast thy gain,
> For thence not far, thou too, like him shalt give
> Thy congregated waters, title—all
> To swell the nobler name of CHESAPEAKE!
> And is not such a scene as this the spell
> That lulls the restless passions into peace?
> Yes. Cold must be the sordid heart, unmoved
> By Nature's bounties: but they cannot fill
> That ardent craving in the mind of man
> For *social intercourse*—the healthful play—
> The moral gem—the light of intellect—
> Communion sweet with those we love!
>
> ("Sketch of a Landscape")

Meanwhile Mrs. Frances Sargent Osgood, the same who for a time figured in the closing years of Poe's life, scolds an unnamed female contemporary who, spoiled by having been too long in city pent, takes insufficient inspiration from the "choral harmony" of nature:

> Go, mar the canvass with distorted face
> Of dog or cat, or worse, profanely mock,
> With gaudy beads, the pure light-painted flower!
> Go, trim your cap, embroider your visite,
> Crocher a purse, do any petty thing!
> But in the name of truth, religion, beauty,
> Let Nature's marvellous mystery alone...
>
> ("A Sermon")

Despite the largely unheeded example of Walt Whitman, American poetry was a long time in getting out from under the notion that in order for everyday experience to be made into the stuff of art, it was necessary to elevate and sanitize it. Thus James Russell Lowell, although a skilled manipulator of imitation Yankee dialect for political purposes, visits France and turns to the High Style to wonder gloomily whether the plebeian, self-made American democrat, "Who, meeting Caesar's self, would slap his back, / Call him 'Old Horse,' and challenge to a drink," will ever rise to the spiritual faith and awe inherent in the medieval cathedral at Chartres:

> Shall he divine no strength unmade of votes,
> Inward, impregnable, found soon as sought,
> Not cognizable of sense, o'er sense supreme?
> Else were he desolate as none before.
>
> ("The Cathedral")

One can only say that whether he does or doesn't, he would be unlikely to think about it in those terms or words. The artificiality of the diction is awesome, and surely far removed from the idiom in which Lowell and his fellow Brahmins ordinarily conversed—"Else were he desolate" indeed! What has happened is that the language of culture and refined sensibility has attained, or more accurately been diluted to, a willed, bloodless ideality, which does not transcend the vernacular fact so much as decline to concede its existence.

The nineteenth-century Anglo-American High Style was predicated upon a shared body of knowledge and a set of agreed-upon community values. As the century came and went, the body of knowledge became so much larger and more complex that proportionally less and less could be shared among the poets and their audience. Moreover, with the decline of religious orthodoxy in the face of scientific knowledge and discovery, the poetry of Ideality, and those who best practiced it, took on a kind of substitute religious status of its own—"Matthew and Waldo, guardians of the faith," as T. S. Eliot put it. If in the eighteenth century the poets had been moralists, by the mid-nineteenth century they were becoming quasi theologians: "Build thee more stately mansions, O my soul."

In the United States the later decades of the nineteenth century were the heyday of the monthly magazines of literature and culture. Readers received not only the successive issues as they appeared but the semiannual bound volumes as well. To maintain liaison with what was now a much-enlarged middle-class reading audience in search of spiritual and artistic enrichment, Victorian-era bards—on this side of the ocean they are referred to as poets of the Genteel Tradition—had to adapt what they could write poems about, and the vocabulary they could use to describe it, to so great an extent that in the hands of lesser practitioners the verse turned into little more than abstract platitudes. Some of the magazine prose of the period remains highly readable a century later, but so completely have tastes in verse changed since then that one may leaf through volume after bound volume of *Scribner's, The Century, Lippincott's, Appleton's, Harper's,* the post-1860s *Atlantic,* etc., without once encountering interesting language in a poem.

As for the major figures, for their part they were hard put to it to keep what they were saying within the limits of what could be comfortably grasped. Robert Browning, for instance, clearly had to execute contortions in order to stay in touch, while Alfred Tennyson, whose talent was essentially for exquisite language, ran out of ideas early on and took to repeating himself, and Matthew Arnold largely ceased writing poems. In the United States, neither of the two major poets at work during the latter half of the century enjoyed a general audience to speak of during their lifetimes. Walt Whitman remained a fringe figure with a reputation for anatomical crudeness, while Emily Dickinson kept her poems unpublished and sewed together in fascicles in her room upstairs.

If poetry was to survive as an art form, clearly something had to be done. Thus was born Modern Poetry and, sequentially but inevitably, the situation in which good poets find themselves today.

When T. S. Eliot published "The Love Song of J. Alfred Prufrock" in *Poetry: A Magazine of Verse* in June 1915, the first three lines announced in effect that henceforth poetry in English was not to be restricted to the nineteenth-century High Style, whether in language or in the way that the style made the poet think:

> Let us go then, you and I,
> When the evening is stretched out against the sky
> Like a patient etherized upon a table.

Stretched out as if under anesthesia? What kind of a poetic image was that? It was not what poetry was expected to do, nor was the language acceptable. Moreover, if one happened to be able to read Italian, and happened to recognize that an epigraph in Italian that preceded the opening lines was from Dante—for the poet did not translate it or identify the source—the implication was that J. Alfred Prufrock's so-called love song was being recited from somewhere in Hell!

It was not, of course, that "Prufrock" did not have predecessors; the importance that has come to be assigned to the publication of that particular poem is retrospective. We did not leap straight from Whittier's "Snow Bound" to "The Waste-Land." Even so, it was the example of Eliot that was foremost, and most influential, in the development of a new idiom, formal without being pretentious, that replaced the poetry of Ideality and made it possible for good poets to deal with something closer to the full range of twentieth-century experience, in the language and attitudes with which they confronted it as citizens.

We have learned to read Eliot so thoroughly over the course of what are now nine decades of Modern Poetry that no doubt it is difficult for today's readers to understand why so many of his own contemporaries, and even more so their elders, found him obscure and Unpoetic. Yet they certainly did, and when "The Waste-Land" appeared (with explanatory footnotes!) in 1922, their bafflement, and for not a few their indignation, was many times augmented.

This is not the place to conduct an investigation into the phenomenon of Modern Poetry, much less an autopsy: after all, though altered over the decades it is neither deceased nor enfeebled. The point is that what poetry did in the United States and England was to jettison the aesthetic and idiom of the poetry of Ideality, and the accompanying assumption that the objective of the poet was to purify everyday experience through elevated diction and lofty thought. Eliot and his contemporaries put aside the role of Everlasting Yea-sayer. They demanded that when composing verse the poet deploy his full intelligence, and not restrict his verse to Poetic subjects. Easily evoked emotional effects would not do.

In a famous pronouncement Eliot declared, "We can only say that it appears likely that poets in our civilization, as it exists at present, must be *difficult*" ("The Metaphysical Poets," 1921). The best poetry of the twentieth century became more and more complex, and more difficult to comprehend than that of the preceding century. It demanded more concentrated attention from its readers, and it offered no easy solutions to hard-to-understand questions. It remains so in a new century.

I do not mean to suggest that poetry has remained unchanged since the advent of Eliot and his contemporaries. Not to change is to die, which is not what has happened. Eliot himself, as High Priest and Grand Panjandrum of the poetry of Modernism, was on the erudite, punctilious side, as he himself recognized and sometimes joked about. Subsequently there has been an overall relaxation in idiom and stance. Poetry has had its fashions and trends, cliques and coteries. As with any new cult there was an in-vocabulary designed to demonstrate membership. For a while it was stylish to be Difficult, to say everything the hard way. There was a High Church literary vogue, whereby Anglican orthodoxy tended to get confused with literary artistry, in part thanks to Eliot's tendencies along that line, as in "A Dialogue on Dramatic Poetry" (1928), in which one of his discussants declares that "the only dramatic satisfaction that I find now is in a High Mass well performed." Conversion to Roman Catholicism also became popular for a time. Sometimes there was a combination of political reaction and literary radicalism within the same poet, of which Ezra Pound was the exemplar. This in turn was succeeded, during the New Left period, by political radicalism, anti-Establishment activism, and in some instances an overt, self-conscious coarseness in idiom. That appears to have eased off, perhaps because it was too monolithic for a medium that depends upon an educated elite for its readership.

In general, the language and attitude of the poetry being published has continued to adhere to the goal that Eliot and his contemporaries set in the 1910s and 1920s, which in "Little Gidding" he characterized as "The common word exact without vulgarity, / The formal word precise but not pedantic" (*Four Quartets,* 1943). So much so that I think it safe to say that not a few of the poems featured in any current issue of *Poetry: A Magazine of Verse* could as appropriately have appeared along with "Prufrock" in the June 1915 number without seeming glaringly out of place. That, it seems to me, constitutes a remarkable continuity.

The price paid for all this has been the constriction, and eventually almost the total loss, of the general literary audience that had bought certain of the nineteenth-century poets in the tens of thousands of copies. It was happening well before the arrival of the television set in the family parlor, but that quickly finished it off.

At the same time, the practice of poetry has spread just about everywhere. The ratio of heat to light is about as efficient as might be hoped. As noted earlier, there is probably more good poetry being written and published than ever before, but on a small, more personal scale. Poetry readings are commonplace, and widely attended. Most recently poets have taken to the Internet in droves. Yet to repeat, there is no national clearinghouse, no real center, no functioning focus of activity. The poets themselves have to arrange everything on their own. In effect it is, You get me a reading on your campus, I'll get you one on mine.

Whether poetry will ever get back in touch with a more general literary audience is moot. Certainly any accommodation it might able to reach will have to be one that will allow it to deal with the more urgent and thorny aspects of human experience, as by the late nineteenth century it largely couldn't any more.

I used to fret about this a good deal, and it continues to rile me that very good poets, whose work I admire greatly and who have been publishing book after book of verse over the years, cannot enjoy more of the fame and the rewards, financial and otherwise, that their work merits. It is annoying, too, to observe, via repeated demonstrations across the years, that in the kind of climate that now prevails, literary politics can count for so much. When not actually at work writing their poetry some poets are masters of the art of self-promotion, while others, including some of the very best, have no gift for it. The last is scarcely a condition peculiar to poets and poetry, but all the same it strikes me that not a few poets are notably skilled at literary maneuvering.

Most important perhaps of all, I remain convinced that poetry is a unique mode of self-knowledge, and intrinsically good to read, so that not to be able to read and enjoy it is a deprivation.

Yet I wonder sometimes whether as far as the art form itself is concerned, poetry may not be better off as now practiced. It is not commercialized, huckstered, glamorized. The people who read it love it, and take it with the seriousness it deserves (which is not the same thing as being portentous and solemn about it). It is not ultrafashionable, and its adherents are not unduly sycophantic. The very fact that it is not commercially exploitable keeps it relatively unalloyed and free from counterfeiting. As with those who aspire to any fine art, many are called but few are chosen. All in all, I am not sure that, for the present at least, the absence of a general audience may not have its real advantages. So long as poetry is flourishing on its own and in its own way, perhaps it doesn't need the kind of help that the entertainment industry could give it.

SLUGGING IT OUT

WITH DEMPSEY AND OTHERS

My ambition when in my teens was to become a sportswriter. I liked sitting in press boxes, at ringside, and at scorer's tables. It gave me a sense of being part of the spectacle, and I enjoyed writing about what happened for the next day's newspaper.

Of course I should have preferred to be an athlete myself. Certain physical limitations, however, having to do with stamina, strength, quickness afoot, agility, balance, coordination, and eyesight, made that improbable, although I tried. Besides, writing was what I liked most of all to do. It was just about the only thing that I was good at, and I couldn't very well have written news stories about myself, anyway.

So I covered the local sports spectrum for the afternoon newspaper, and although receiving no pay for doing so I got to be close to where the action was—even, on one notable occasion when seated just below an elevated prize-ring at the Golden Gloves, having the sheet of paper I was writing on sprinkled with blood when one of the pugilists landed a glancing blow upon the snout of his opponent up against the ropes. There's glory for you.

In those days, whatever our teachers and parents might say to the contrary, sports were what counted. The High School of Charleston (boys only) had no literary magazine, no yearbook, and no clubs or societies in which dabbling in the belles lettres was encouraged. All it had was a monthly newspaper, of which in my senior year I was the editor. But there were varsity teams in all the major and most of the minor sports, not including soccer. Nobody played soccer back then in our part of the country, any more than lacrosse or ice hockey, which were sports that one might read about in the *New York Times* or the *New York Herald-Tribune,* but not in South Carolina.

What we did have was boxing, which in the 1920s and 1930s was a major high school and college sport. There was also professional boxing in town—a card each week at Sullivan's Bowl, and Golden Gloves and other competitions. This was before the advent of television. There was prizefighting in all American cities of any size, and national championship boxing matches were reported at great length in the newspapers. A fight for the heavyweight title was at least as noteworthy an event, with as extensive a promotional buildup, as the World Series or the Super Bowl is today.

I am moved to the above reflections upon reading a biography, *A Flame of Pure Fire: Jack Dempsey and the Roaring '20s,* by Roger Kahn (1999). Kahn is known as author of one of the best books about major league baseball, *The Boys of Summer,* but one of his objectives here is to demonstrate that, far more so than Babe Ruth, William Harrison Dempsey (1895–1983) was the dominant American athlete of the Mencken-Harding-Capone Age. He was capable of earning a million dollars a year, while Ruth's income never came close to that. Kahn's point is that in an era when the renown of athletic heroes was at apogee, the heavyweight champ, not the home run hitter, ranked first. The same held true for the other famous performers of the day, such as Bobby Jones and Walter Hagen in golf, Bill Tilden in tennis, and Red Grange in football. None of them could draw spectators or produce revenue to compare with Dempsey.

What is also interesting is that in the three-quarters of a century since then, those other sports have maintained or enhanced their respectability, meanwhile being joined by basketball and, to a degree, soccer, while boxing on the contrary has lost a great deal of its general appeal and is no longer considered an appropriate form of recreation among the Great American Middle Class. Those who box are recruited almost wholly from among the street fighters of large cities, where the gymnasiums and youth centers sponsor organized fisticuffs, as distinguished from the unsupervised variety, as a form of social rehabilitation for the underprivileged. So complete has the eclipse of the fight game been among other and more fortunate sectors of our citizenry that I doubt that many people not in their sixties and seventies realize that there was ever a time when, at numerous American colleges and universities and most preparatory and high schools of any size, boxing was a major competitive sport.

Reading Kahn on Dempsey had the effect of inciting my curiosity, however, and I went searching in the stacks at our local university library to see what else might be available concerning the practice of the Manly Art of Modified Mayhem, as boxing used to be called back when it was a respectable activity like major league baseball or quoits. I won't say that what I discovered touched off any nostalgia within my bosom, but it was interesting to read how various prose masters past and present have handled the fight game.

When one thinks of boxing in literary terms, it is Hemingway who immediately comes to mind: "Robert Cohn was once middleweight boxing champion of Princeton. Do not think that I am very much impressed by that as a boxing title, but it meant a lot to Cohn." In actuality, as Joyce Carol Oates notes, Hemingway wrote relatively little about boxing. The point, however, is that were Hemingway beginning his career today, a character such as Cohn, like Harold Loeb, who inspired him, would never be accorded such credentials, and neither would Hemingway challenge Morley Callaghan to bouts with Scott Fitzgerald as inattentive timekeeper, or otherwise seek to further his artistic renown with the help of boxing gloves. To exhibit maleness in time of peace he would have been forced to rely entirely upon field and Gulf Stream, or perhaps karate. (One can readily envision Papa in kung-fu garb.)

These days the leading literary devotees of the ring are Oates, a nonparticipant, and Norman Mailer, who is not otherwise a sports fan and who views boxing much as Oates does, if out of a different need—as masculine aggression unveneered by the refinements of bat, ball, racket, or assault rifle.

Roger Kahn reports that Jack Dempsey told him in conversation that when in the early 1920s he visited Paris, he did some sparring there, but "there was one fellow I wouldn't mix it with. That was Ernest Hemingway. He was about twenty-five or so and in good shape, and I was getting so I could read people, or anyway men, pretty well. I had this sense that

Hemingway, who really thought he could box, would come out of the corner like a madman. To stop him, I would have to hurt him badly. I didn't want to do that to Hemingway. That's why I never sparred with him." For his part, Hemingway professed not to care for Dempsey; why this was I do not know, though one can make a conjecture or two. In any event it is not important. What does seem evident from Kahn's biography is that Dempsey was a more modest and likable fellow than Hemingway, and that fewer demons drove him.

The recruitment of professional boxers mainly from among the disadvantaged and deprived is hardly a new development; on the contrary, it was ever thus, for all that it was once a popular middle-class recreation. With only a few exceptions, those who have contended for professional boxing championships have done so not only because they were gifted at it, but because they needed money. If we look at a prizefight on television nowadays, it is likely to be between or among blacks, Latinos, or perhaps Asians, for the obvious reason that it is a way for an uneducated, vocationally unskilled, hungry youth to earn some and very occasionally a great deal of money very quickly. Why otherwise would anyone be willing to put up with the relentless brutality, highly unsavory conditions, and general sleaze associated with the fight game?

Prizefighting developed, first in England then over here, along with the Industrial Revolution and the growth of cities and proletarian populations. In the late nineteenth century and well into the twentieth the leading battlers were Irish—John L. Sullivan, who could "lick any man in the house," Gentleman Jim Corbett, Bob Fitzsimmons, Philadelphia Jack O'Brien, Kid McKoy, Terry McGovern, Mickey Walker, Gene Tunney, Tommy Loughran, Jimmy McLarnin, James J. Braddock, Billy Conn, and others—and Jewish—Benny Leonard, Battling Levinsky, Lew Tendler, Abe Attell, Harry Greb, Maxie Rosenbloom, Barney Ross, Max Baer, and so on. From the 1920s onward there were the Italians, Poles, and other immigrant groups—Tony Canzoneri, Jack Sharkey (Zukauskas), Melio Bettina, Babe Risko (Pulaski), Jake La Motta, Rocky Graziano, Rocky Marciano, Willie Pep (Papaleo), Rocky Kansas (Tozzo), Joey Giardello, Carmen Basilio, Fritzie Zivic, Joe and Vince Dundee (Lazzaro), Willie Pastrano, Al Hostak, Gus Lesnevich, and more.

There were always good black fighters, but they were systematically discriminated against. When Jack Johnson won the heavyweight championship there began a widespread search for a "White Hope," culminating in Jess Willard taking the title in 1915. Many of the best fighters around—Peter Jackson, Sam Langford, Joe Gans, Harry Wills, Joe Jeannette—were never allowed to contend for the championship because they were black. The advent of Joe Louis in the mid-1930s changed that, and since 1960 the heavyweight kings have all been black. Meanwhile the Latinos have been coming along, especially in the lighter weight classifications, as a glance at the listing of current champions in the *World Almanac* makes clear.

Jack Dempsey was no exception to the economic pattern. He grew to manhood in Colorado under very rough circumstances. He borrowed his first name from Jack Dempsey the "Nonpareil," who held the middleweight title in the 1880s and died an alcoholic and a bum in 1895 at age thirty-three. As a pro fighter the Manassa Mauler—his place of birth was Manassa, Colorado—fought early, in streets, barrooms, mining camps, wherever he could pick up a few dollars; he worked in the mines, hopped freights, rode the rods, married a piano-playing whore, and as a pugilist began to prosper only after hooking up with a manager, John Leo McKernan, known professionally as Doc Kearns. A fast-talking, less than scrupulous operator, Kearns pocketed half of Dempsey's earnings plus costs, but got him numerous fights, which Dempsey customarily won by knockouts. By the late 1910s he was in a position to challenge for the heavyweight title.

Dempsey won the championship from Jess Willard in 1919, after which he took up residence in California and tried some movie work. In what was apparently an attempted shakedown by his now-divorced wife, who had returned to her chosen profession, he was accused and tried retroactively in a federal court for draft evasion during the recently completed War to End All Wars, but was swiftly exonerated by the jury.

In 1921, in Jersey City, Dempsey knocked out Georges Carpentier in the fourth round of a fight that drew more than eighty thousand spectators, or about four times as many as had watched the Willard fight in Toledo two years before. The sports explosion of the twenties was on. The contest attracted international attention. In England, George Bernard Shaw predicted a victory by Carpentier, willingly "staking my reputation for knowing what I write about"—an ambivalent claim at that. As Roger Kahn notes, Shaw would give another demonstration of his wisdom a decade later when, after interviewing Josef Stalin in the Kremlin, he would describe him as "simply a party functionary and nothing more. Given one week's notice, Stalin can be removed from office."

The money rolled in, Dempsey returned to Hollywood and the movies, bedding a variety of stars of the silent screen, and he and Kearns spent lavishly, in the time-honored fashion of the poor boy from across the tracks who becomes suddenly and enormously rich. He defended his title against Tommy Gibbons in a promotional fiasco arranged by Kearns in Shelby, Montana, then later that year—1923—came the wild brawl with Luis Angel Firpo, the "Wild Bull of the Pampas," at the Polo Grounds in New York City. Dempsey knocked Firpo down seven times in the first round, then Firpo knocked Dempsey out of the ring and into press row. Dempsey scrambled and was pushed back into the ring, and knocked Firpo out in the second round. Afterward Firpo protested that the help given to his opponent to regain the ring was illegal—as indeed it was. "So many writers pushed Dempsey into the ring that it looked like he was getting a back massage," Firpo declared. The protest was disallowed.

The champion returned to Hollywood for more movies and acquired another wife, this time Estelle Taylor, a movie actress experienced at romance both on and off the screen. Estelle didn't like Doc Kearns, who didn't like her and who feared rightly that Dempsey was being diverted from keeping up his boxing training. Dempsey had been growing suspicious, likewise rightly, that Kearns was regularly siphoning off more than his proper share of Dempsey's earnings. Although without much formal education, Dempsey was an intelligent man, and he decided thereafter to do his own managing. It was an old and familiar story in the fight game: the manager assists the pugilist into the financial Promised Land, after which the pugilist comes to resent both the manager's sizable share of the spoils and his continuing assumption that the now-matured fighter requires someone to do all his professional thinking for him.

In Dempsey's instance Kearns seemed to believe, as Kahn writes, "that he had an unspoken lifetime agreement with Dempsey. Half the proceeds. Half the proceeds for eternity." (Kearns operated out of New York City, where state boxing law specifically limited the manager's share to one-third of the fighter's earnings.) Still, while Kearns's bookkeeping was on the highly suspect side, he was skilled at handling his fighter's strategy and tactics during the course of a fight, and in what was to follow he might well have made a difference in the outcome.

Because their written contract was good through August 1926, Dempsey held off defending his title for close to three years, during which time he became ring-rusty, as they say. It was his intention to take on Harry Wills in Michigan City, Indiana, but the promoter did not come across with the promised guarantee. In New York City another and more solvent operator, Tex Rickard, had some years earlier promoted several contests with black fighters which had done less than spectacularly at the box office, and he was dead set against the champion taking on Wills, who was black. Dempsey has since been depicted as having been afraid to fight a black foe, but it would appear that his concerns were less ethnic than monetary. In any event, he fought Gene Tunney instead, and on September 23, 1926, lost his championship by being decisively outpointed in ten rounds at Philadelphia before 120,757 paying customers, the gate receipts totaling $1,895,733 (multiply by about ten to approximate today's equivalent, not including pay-TV rights). The total take at Dempsey's victory over Jess Willard in 1919 had been $452,223.

Dempsey then knocked out Jack Sharkey, and the stage was set for the famous "long count" in Chicago. He took on the new champion at Soldier Field in Chicago, September 22, 1927. When the fight began Tunney stuck to clever boxing, keeping away from Dempsey while occasionally landing solid punches of his own, and was well ahead on points when abruptly, in the seventh round, Dempsey's left fist found the range. Tunney faltered, upon which a series of well-aimed shots sent him to the canvas.

Dempsey stood by to observe the count. The referee, Dave Barry, instructed him to go to a neutral corner, as specified by the playing rules. "I stay," said Dempsey. So Barry escorted him to the furthest corner, then returned to the stricken Tunney. By that time the official timekeeper had counted to five, but Barry began his count at one. When it reached eight, Tunney rose to his feet, having been on the canvas for from fourteen to eighteen seconds; estimates vary according to the dudgeon of the estimator. Thereafter Tunney stayed beyond reach of the frustrated Dempsey.

"I honestly thought Dempsey was going to kill me," Tunney afterward told one newspaperman.

Dempsey lost mobility, and in the eighth round Tunney landed a combination that briefly downed his tiring opponent. The champion likewise stood close by to observe, but the referee only ignored his presence. "Watching this moment on videotape," Roger Kahn writes, "one is consumed by outrage. Two knockdowns, one round apart, and two different sets of rules. The explanation, I believe, is not complicated. In my tape of Chicago 1927, I am looking at a crooked referee."

Maybe. The time was the twenties, the city was Chicago, and in civilian life the referee, appointed over Dempsey's representatives' objections, operated a speakeasy, an undertaking not sanctioned by the law. The Boo Boo Hoff mob from Philadelphia was backing Tunney and may even have had a stake in his proprietorship, while the locally based Al Capone caucus was pro-Dempsey in its wagering. Dempsey's subsequent protest was rejected by the National Boxing Association, however. In any event, nobody in a position to know has ever seriously suggested that either of the fighters was less than totally committed to winning.

As a prizefighter Dempsey was renowned for the fury of his attack and the power of his punching. Within the ring he was savage and unrelenting; outside it he was courteous and friendly, and enjoyed the company of others. Until he lost the heavyweight championship, Kahn says, he was largely disliked by the fight-watching multitudes. After the defeat by Tunney, however, he became very popular, retaining public favor until his death in 1983 at age eighty-seven. For years he operated a restaurant on Broadway between Forty-ninth and Fiftieth Streets, until the neighborhood grew too tawdry and even dangerous. He was married four times in all, lastly and most successfully at age sixty-two. Known for his generosity to former associates and acquaintances, he ended his days in comfort but not wealthy.

When Dempsey fought Carpentier in Jersey City in 1921, twelve U.S. senators and ninety congressmen were on hand to watch. From ringside Irvin S. Cobb contributed a front-page account to the *New York Times*, deposing as follows: "The arts, the sciences, the drama, commerce, politics, the bench, the bar, the great newly risen bootlegging industry—all these have all sent their pink, their pick and their perfection to grace this great occasion." Today's clientele at a fight for the heavyweight championship would be very different. The bout itself would be taking place in Las Vegas before an audience of well-heeled fight fans drawn from the ranks of the sporting and mass entertainment industry, totally minus the politicos, socialites, brokers, and artists. Elsewhere in the country true believers would be watching on closed-circuit television, having paid premium fees for the privilege. The vast majority of sports fans would read the results in the morning paper, if indeed they bothered to do so. For boxing no longer enchants most folk, and the long trail leading from Jack Dempsey to Evander Holyfield, the world-title holder as I write this, is all downward, in recent years precipitously so. Roger Kahn's entertaining and well-written book—a very good job, though accompanied by too much facilely compiled Roaring 20s material having nothing to do with prizefighting— chronicles the vanished pomps of yesteryear, as they say.

There have been numerous accounts of the Dempsey era before Kahn's. One of the best, written for the *New Yorker* magazine in the late 1940s and published as a book, *White Hopes and Other Tigers* (1951), is by John Lardner, son of Ring and a longtime sportswriter. Lardner doesn't have much to say about the two Dempsey-Tunney battles; he concentrates on the search for a pugilist to protect the honor of the Caucasian race after Jack Johnson took the heavyweight championship from Tommy Burns in 1908. Not until 1915, when Jess Willard, a very large but not notably agile fellow known as the Pottawatomie Giant, won the title with a twenty-sixth-round knockout of Johnson in Havana, Cuba, could the Caucasian race supposedly breathe easy again.

Johnson afterward claimed that he threw the fight in an effort to secure leniency on a trumped-up charge of having violated the Mann Act, which was preventing him from returning to his native land, and there is a photo of him lying on his back in the ring, supposedly unconscious and being counted out, even as he holds a gloved hand and forearm over his eyes to shield them from the sunlight overhead. The photographic evidence is by no means conclusive, however, and in Lardner's words, "In any case, the white hope era ended then and there."

Lardner then describes the rise of Dempsey and his manager Doc Kearns, his capture of the title from Willard in 1919, and his subsequent victorious battles with Carpentier, Gibbons, and Firpo. Lardner's style is sardonic and witty, with a ready ear for the telling comment by practitioners and their colleagues. Of Jim Coffey, an Irish white hope of the period, for example, Lardner quotes manager Dumb Dan Morgan on "the law of jaws": Coffey "was a great prospect as long as he ate poor man's food, like chuck steak, that keeps the jaw tough. But he made some money and started eating porterhouse, and his jaws went to hell."

Lardner's pièce de résistance, in a book of splendid episodes, is his account of the Dempsey-Gibbons fight, staged in Shelby, Montana, in 1923, in which that very small western town, made prosperous by an oil boom, sought to establish itself on the map by staging a contest for the heavyweight championship. Before it ended, Jack Kearns had collected close to $300,000 for Dempsey and himself, the Gibbons entourage had received nothing, and the four banks of the Shelby area had closed their doors. Lardner characterizes the episode as "the Sack of Shelby."

The writer who wrote most consistently about boxing, mainly for the old *New Yorker,* was A. J. Liebling. Starting in the 1930s, and with a break during the war as a correspondent, he composed numerous installments of what he called "The Sweet Science," a term borrowed from his favorite book, an early nineteenth-century chronicle of prizefighting by an Irishman named Pierce Egan. Many of Liebling's best pieces are collected in his own chronicle, also entitled *The Sweet Science* (1956). Joe Liebling was the consummate literary New York native son, widely cultured but streetwise and suspicious, and, to quote one of his admirers, he "loved to inflate a sentence, then release it like a helium balloon and watch it skitter across a page." Thus Liebling on the reluctance of sparring partners to damage each other when appearing in actual bouts: "A kind of guild fellowship holds them together, and they pepper each other's elbows with merry abandon, grunting with pleasure like hippopotamuses in a beer vat." The trick is to mingle the formal, even the learned, with the vernacular, delighting the scholarly reader yet making it clear that the author is committed to the earth earthy, or more precisely, the urbs urbane.

Liebling took joy in recording the speech of the inhabitants of Stillman's Gym, a much-chronicled training arena on Eighth Avenue between Fifty-fourth and Fifty-fifth Streets where the boxing fraternity then tended to gather. His all-time favorite elocutionist was the noted trainer and ringside damage-repairman Whitey Bimstein, as in the following on the blessed memory of the Boston Tar Baby, Sam Langford: "'What a difference from the kids today,' the schoolman said. 'I have a kid in a bout last night and he can't even count. Every time he hook the guy is open for a right, and I tell him, "Go twicet, go twicet!" But he would go oncet and lose the guy. I don't know what they teach them in school.'"

Unlike the daily pressmen or even the weekly stylists for the newsmagazines, Liebling wrote to no urgent deadline, and the attractions of a more leisurely life permeate his prose. He is easily diverted from the immediate subject, and, to adopt his own way of putting things, goes wandering off Laurence Sterne–fashion with Aunt Dinah and her coachman into the heart of the planetary system before returning to the matter at hand.

Fred Warner, in an afterword to *A Neutral Corner,* a collection of hitherto-uncollected Liebling boxing articles edited by Warner and James Barbour and published in 1990, more than a quarter century after Liebling's death in 1963, expresses doubt as to whether many of those who read such pieces in the *New Yorker* "cared much about boxing. Most of his readers accepted exposure to a brutal and alien sport because they loved good prose." This I think might very likely be true were Liebling writing today, but Liebling in his own heyday could count upon no small number of his readers being reasonably well informed about the outcomes of the major bouts he chronicled. They would already know who won and who lost, and so would not be impatient while he conducted them on a meandering narrative in which there is an abundance of whimsy. Here for example is a lively specimen describing the bout between Archie Moore and Rocky Marciano in the early 1950s:

> So Ahab had his harpoon in the Whale. He had hit him right if ever I saw a boxer hit right, with a classic brevity and conciseness. Marciano stayed down for two seconds. I do not know what took place in Mr. Moore's breast when he saw him get up. He may have felt, for the moment, like Don Giovanni when the Commendatore's statue grabbed at him—startled because he thought he had killed the guy

already—or like Ahab when he saw the Whale take down Fedallah, harpoons and all. Anyway, he hesitated a couple of seconds, and that was reasonable. A man who took nine to come up after a punch like that would be doing well, and the correct tactic would be to go straight in and finish him. But a fellow who came up on two was so strong he would bear investigation.

To get the full savor it is necessary to know in advance that Archie Moore is an aging but still puissant light-heavy who has come out of his normal weight class to take on the undefeated heavyweight champion, and also that Moore puts up a heroic battle but ends up getting knocked out. Early in the fight he lands a knockdown punch of his own that by the lights of all the challenger's previous ring experience should have stunned Marciano, setting him up for a knockout—only to have the champion, massively built and strong as an ox, come bouncing to his feet at the count of two. It is at that moment in the fight that Moore realizes, for the first time, what he is up against. So, instead of wading in as is customary to follow up what should have been the swift annihilation of a near-helpless opponent, he hesitates.

A few pages earlier Liebling remarks that "the fight had caught the public imagination, ever sensitive to a meeting between Hubris and Nemesis, as the boys on the quarterlies would say." He thereby thumbs a glove at the Intellectuals. This is quintessentially a William Shawn–era *New Yorker* gambit, possible only on the assumption that there is a reading public that follows the fight news, reads both Edmund Wilson and Red Smith, listens to Mozart, and will grasp the significance of Marciano springing to his feet at the count of two without the need for Liebling to cite Aristotle on Recognition.

At the same time, however, he doesn't want to risk alienating his readers by making the Real World of Stillman's Gym and the fans at the Garden appear too sordid for aesthetic contemplation. He can develop the high-cultural metaphors as they become appropriate, but he had better not go too far with the Lower Depths realism. So he tends to omit such motifs as the taste for cruelty that not a few of his heroes of the prize ring exhibit, and he has little to say about the financial exploitation of the ghetto-reared, half-educated brawlers by the managers and promoters who book the fights and collect the purses. The brain-damaged ex-gladiator looking for handouts who shuffles along Jacobs Beach (so called because of the presence in the neighborhood of the promoter Mike Jacobs's office) figures scarcely at all in his annals of "The Sweet Science."

The Sonny Liston that Liebling describes as he goes to work on Floyd Patterson is not the same man described by Joyce Carol Oates—"something so elemental and primitive that it cannot be named." Little in Liston's portrait as rendered by Liebling would suggest that he was, as Oates points out, one of numerous children of a sharecropping family, who when a teenager got enough to eat only while in jail, was arrested nineteen times and served two prison terms, one of them for armed robbery, worked as an enforcer for a union, and not long after his ring career ended would die of an overdose of heroin at age thirty-eight.

Oates, a notable fight aficionado, is not an admirer of Liebling on boxing. He offers, she declares, a "relentlessly jokey, condescending, and occasionally racist attitude toward his subject." Perhaps—but Liebling's so-called racism seems to me little more than the reflexive humor of a time and place. No one who is familiar with the "Wayward Press" pieces he was also writing regularly for the *New Yorker* in the 1940s and 1950s would accuse him of an insensitivity to the cause of civil rights, which in Liebling's time and place is what mattered. I have the sense that Oates simply doesn't care for any kind of jesting about what for her are conducted tours into the Inferno.

It is true, however, that in writing about boxing Liebling is portraying life in the Lower Depths. He applies no formula to what he observes there, but psychologically he accepts a basic assumption of late-nineteenth-century literary naturalism: that life in the slums comes closest to the basic human condition, being least gilded over with social artifice and ornament and therefore nearest to the elemental struggle for survival within a hostile natural environment. His preoccupation with the prize ring seems something like Teddy Roosevelt's for the strenuous life: the fascination of a bookishly inclined person who from his younger days on has disciplined himself to take part in it. About the motivation, mores, and nonpugilistic activities of those involved, the less said the better. Or so I read Liebling.

Oates, by contrast, goes relentlessly into the whys and wherefores. She tells us, in her intense little book, *On Boxing* (1987), that to prepare herself for its writing she watched the tapes of two prizefights in which the losers were mauled so viciously that they died afterward. The violence must not be blinked at; the savagery is the source of the fascination; and the tie-in with economic deprivation and the Survival of the Fittest is direct and unadorned. Most of those who box professionally "are the sons of impoverished ghetto neighborhoods in which anger, if not fury, is appropriate—rather more, perhaps, than Christian meekness and self-abnegation."

It is not the sociology of boxing, however, but its Jungian underpinning that engages her principal attention. The boxing match, she suggests, "is the very language, the more terrifying for being so stylized, of mankind's collective aggression; its ongoing historical madness." It is, finally, the enactment of a ritual; "man is *in extremis,* performing an atavistic rite or *agon* for the mysterious solace of those who can participate only vicariously in such drama: the drama of life in the flesh." The finality of its outcome, the way in which the careers of even its most successful practitioners can come abruptly to a halt, strikes her as providing tragic inevitability, as if Birnam Wood were arriving at Dunsinane: "boxing in its greatest moments suggests the bloody fifth acts of classic tragedies, in which that mysterious element we call 'plot' achieves closure."

Oates does not set out to chronicle notable bouts, and so unlike Joe Liebling and most other writers about boxing she feels no obligation to report what happens over the course of a particular fight. For that reason a statement she makes at the outset of her book seems puzzling, in the light of what will then follow: "For if you have seen five hundred boxing matches you have seen five hundred boxing matches and their common denominator, which certainly exists, is not of primary interest to you." But it is precisely their common denominator—what as human activity they *mean*—that concerns her in her book. I suppose that what she is getting at is that when she is in attendance at a fight or watching it replayed on film or tape, it is *that* fight, not the pursuit of any kind of an ideal Platonic *agon* of which it is merely one instance, that commands her attention. Thus her book, while indubitably an effort to understand and to explain why the fight game fascinates her, is an afterthought, written to answer for herself an oft-asked question posed by others: "How can you enjoy so brutal a sport?" She doesn't "enjoy" it, she insists, it isn't "invariably brutal," and she doesn't think of it as a sport. It appears to offer what the Fat Boy would seek to accomplish in the *Pickwick Papers:* "I wants to make your flesh creep."

After reading and admiring, if also being somewhat appalled by, Oates's self-inquiry into the lure of boxing, I found it a distinct change of pace to come upon Phil Berger's *Punch Lines: Berger on Boxing* (1993), a selection of well-written pieces about fighters and others involved in the industry, by the boxing writer of the *New York Times.* No authorial self-scrutiny goes on here. Thoroughly schooled in the milieu of the prize ring as encountered in the Age of Television, the author sees it as no part of his job to explore his own emotional involvement in what those he writes about do for a living. If for Joe Liebling prizefighting was low comedy, and for Joyce Carol Oates it is, or can be, tragedy, for Berger it is spectacle. What manner of men are those who engage in it? he asks, and proceeds to investigate.

The particular kind of personality resulting when a largely inchoate, or in any event unreflective, young man, reared in direst poverty and steeped in street combat, finds himself suddenly wealthy and sought after—this is what most fascinates Berger. Naturally this principally involves blacks, although one doesn't feel that Berger thinks of himself as dealing in racial distinctions. His most interesting writings are about Leon Spinks and Mike Tyson, both of whom were for a time all-conquering, then saw their gilded empires dismantled. In both instances a damaging flaw in character makes the subsequent collapse inevitable. Berger senses almost from the outset that there are two sides to the sometimes shy Tyson, and the other and darker exposure features the savage aggressor, the sadistic inflicter of pain not only upon his ring opponents but also upon women and small animals. Berger doesn't actually use the word *schizophrenia,* but clearly he believes that contradictory personalities wage full-scale war within Tyson's psyche, and so he is in no way surprised when within a few years the one-time heavyweight champ ends up in the penitentiary for raping a participant in a beauty pageant.

The sequence on Leon Spinks is if anything even more appalling, for there is the definite sense that the man has a screw loose in his cranium, and his irresponsibility is the result of a frightening, wild-animal-like irrationality. He is, in sum, both *stupid* and *crazy.* The disaster that inevitably results is made all the more poignant by a piece on Leon Spinks's teenage son by a common-law spouse, who clearly inherits his father's skills and also his brains. Displaying definite talent as a boxer, he never develops it, for he is gunned to death in a youth gang fracas. For counterpoint there is a piece on Leon Spinks's brother Michael, who also wins the heavyweight title. Possessing nothing like Leon's color and flair, he is, in Berger's words, "a decent and straightforward individual who has shown the discipline and toughmindedness to succeed as a pro" and is smart enough to take care of himself and hold on to his earnings.

What I found, when caught up in Oates's inquiries into what went on inside her while watching this fight or that, and also when wading through Norman Mailer's impassioned metapolitics of the prize ring as Revolution, was that there were times when I needed a reality check, so to speak—whereupon I read a relevant essay in Phil Berger's book. Not that what Oates or even Mailer wrote was invalid as speculative inquiry—but those involved were, after all, certain real-life people engaged in earning a living in the prize ring, not transcendent figures of fable.

When writing about boxing, Norman Mailer, as might be suspected, goes at his prose as if engaged in slugging it out with The Great Antagonist—perhaps Hemingway, perhaps Victor Hugo, perhaps John Updike; who is to say? In his book about the Muhammad Ali–George Foreman heavyweight title fight in Zaire in 1974, *The Fight* (1975), Mailer writes of himself in the third person, even though conceding that to do so "irritated critics. They spoke of ego trips and the unattractive dimensions of his narcissism." As when, to bring an end to his narrative, he tells of playing a multidice board game with the airline stewardesses while flying back to the United States. Some weeks later he remembers the incident and "thinking of it, he sent each of the girls an autographed copy of the softcover edition of *Marilyn* and expressed the hope that they would think his ability to write was somewhat greater than his flair for dice."

A few pages before that comes a reverie on Black Power, including a 750-word excerpt from a speech by Louis Farrakhan, loaded with the rhetoric of racial hatred and extolling Elijah Muhammad, not Martin Luther King Jr., as the one reliable prophet and messiah, and so on. On the basis of what he has seen happen in the ring at Zaire, Mailer decides that the true strength of Ali, as a communicant of Elijah, lies in his belief in the Nation of Islam, and the resulting link with the Arabs is menacing:

> No, Norman had the uneasy intuition that sooner or later his admiration for Ali could change to the respect one felt for a powerful and dedicated enemy. No turn was too sinuous for the tricks of history, and no dimension necessarily too small for the future growth of Muhammad Ali. They had bestowed upon him, after all, a name with a great weight upon it. The original Ali was the adopted son of the Prophet Muhammad. Now a modern Muhammad Ali might become the leader of his people. It was well for Muhammad Ali that he believed in predestination and surrender to the will of God.

Sad to say, it didn't happen that way for poor Ali. When his (white) physician warned him to get out of boxing, he fired the physician—and today, several decades later, the once articulate and alert master of the ring increasingly resembles a zombie. The Nation of Islam has since made no noticeable difference in either the heavyweight rankings or the election returns. But by blending a prizefight with the hostilities at Megiddo or Armageddon, Mailer came up with a gorgeous apocalyptic vision to divert him while en route home.

Joyce Carol Oates, who much admires Mailer's writing about boxing, interprets him as follows. Mailer "cannot establish a connection between himself and the boxers: he tries heroically but he cannot understand them and so he is forever excluded from what, unthinkingly, they represent: an ideal (because unthinking, unforced) masculinity. It is this recognition of his exclusion—an exclusion very nearly as complete as, say, the exclusion of a woman from boxing's codified world—that allows for the force of Mailer's vision. And since the great champions of our time have been black, Mailer's preoccupation with masculinity is a preoccupation with blackness as well." Ali's personality awes Mailer, and the Black Power he propounds threatens to become a cosmic force, like the French Revolution or the Internet. Even so, it does not follow that when Muhammad Ali knocked out George Foreman in eight rounds, the social statics of Louis Farrakhan were thereby enacted.

Budd Schulberg, a different kind of writer from Norman Mailer, writes for a middlebrow audience, and comes to boxing not in search of reality but because he views it as a form of showbiz and is at home in it. Having grown to manhood among the klieg lights—his father was a greatly successful Hollywood producer—Schulberg took to the ring milieu while yet a mere lad. The sense of exclusion by virtue of the unthinking masculinity of prizefighters that Oates believes bedevils Mailer would never perturb Budd Schulberg. Without so much as a moment's doubt he assumes his membership in the fight community, and writes unself-consciously from within the arena.

In a collection of his boxing pieces dating from the early 1950s through the mid-1990s, *Sparring with Hemingway and Other Legends of the Fight Game* (1995), he offers his interpretation of a bout for the heavyweight championship when genuinely first-rate pugilists are matched:

> ...these primitive two-man wars have magic for me, recalling the myth of man as a simple, indomitable fighting animal, the most ferocious and capable of all such animals on earth, in there along with only the speed and force of his fisted hands, the durability of his jaw and ribs, belly and skin, the speed and endurance of his legs, plus the decisive intangibles, character, intelligence, spirit, pride—only these for weapons.

This is not to say that Schulberg is uncritical of the fight game. On the contrary, he is outraged by mismatches, fixes, machinations of any kind. He can get sufficiently worked up on occasion to advocate federal regulation, close medical certification and supervision, pensions, reforms, legislation. Yet any talk of abolishing professional boxing is anathema to him. What boxing needs is reformation, not abolition, he insists. He castigates the American Medical Association "lobby" for declaring that on any level the prize ring is inherently deleterious to health. This was five years before Mike Tyson, during a thwarted effort to regain the title, took a bite out of Evander Holyfield's ear, thereby indicating, according to some commentators, that his preferred diet was cauliflower.

Lest it be thought that the United Kingdom, where prizefighting as we know it today got its start, has forsaken the Manly Art, I suggest a reading of *On the Ropes: Boxing as a Way of Life,* by Geoffrey Beattie (1996). The author spent considerable time in Sheffield, once a center of steel manufacture but now fallen upon crass times, and in particular at a training gymnasium operated by a transplanted Irishman, Brendan Ingle, who encourages the young to box and manages the careers of some of them. The clientele will match any in similar American institutions, and the milieu outside is sufficiently depressed to compare with the best that New York City, Chicago, or Detroit can offer in slum conditions.

Brendan Ingle—who has signs posted about his establishment reading "Boxing Can Damage Your Health!"—is a likable character with a total zeal for his profession. After several near misses with fighters who aspired to championships but couldn't quite make it, Ingle now has a protégé of Yemeni parentage, "Prince" Naseem Hamed, who is ready to challenge for the bantamweight championship of the world as recognized by one of the competing sanctioning groups. The young man, who was taken in off the streets by Ingle at age seven, has patterned himself after Muhammad Ali, including his boastfulness. His earnings are now in the millions, and he is also, as the author suggests, well along in arrogance and growing away from his patron and preceptor. But not just yet, and when at the close of the book Naseem wins the title, Brendan Ingle, after many years of trying, has his world champ and 25 percent of the proceeds. (As I wrote this, four years later, Prince Naseem Hamed was internationally renowned and had successfully defended the world featherweight championship for the umpteenth time. Ingle had long since been discarded.)

Earlier in the year that Naseem won his initial title, Ingle assisted at ringside at a fight between the World Boxing Association super-middleweight champion, Nigel Benn, and Gerald McClellan, which Ingle describes as "the greatest fight I've ever seen in a British ring." A few hours afterward, McClellan ended up in a hospital with neurosurgeons striving to remove a clot from his brain. It was, Ingle tells Beattie,

> boxing at its most sophisticated, crude, barbaric, enchanting, skillful—all at the same time. Boxing is a serious business. I teach my lads how to take precautions—how to survive in the ring. But I remind them that they're not playing marbles in there. That fight was what life was all about—it was Benn coming back from the brink of nearly getting killed, and surviving. It was McClellan coming back from

the brink of nearly getting killed and surviving . . . Just remember, you don't begin to live until you begin to die. That's well worth remembering.

Much though Beattie admires Ingle's devotion to his profession, the author has his doubts. But Ingle's justification is not greatly different in logic from Budd Schulberg on George Foreman coming back at the age of forty-two to lose a close decision to Evander Holyfield for the heavyweight championship in 1991: "If Big George never fights again, he's given us exactly what we need in these days of cynicism, when the underclass, the lower class, and even troubled members of the middle class are groping to find a way." Or Joyce Carol Oates's fascination with boxing as "the very language, the more terrifying for being so stylized, of mankind's collective aggression; its ongoing historical madness."

The price that boxing can exact from all too many of its practitioners is made very clear by a perceptive ex-journalist, Ralph Wiley, in *Serenity: A Boxing Memoir* (1989). Wiley's title is, at the very least, ambivalent. He opens with a prologue containing the assertion, "In spite of their circumstances fighters have serenity to a greater degree than ordinary people. Whether fighters gain their serenity because they face down life and death or because the sense to worry has been knocked clean out of their heads, I don't know. They may lose many things by the time they stop fighting, but they remain serene." But he closes only after he has shown us a Sugar Ray Robinson who is in a gathering stupor and a Muhammad Ali—this was a decade ago—already showing an odd torpidity, even though his physical reflexes still appeared to be sound. "Damage, specifically brain damage, is what boxing is all about," he writes. "Boxing is assault and battery with deadly weapons called the fists of man. Ali's brain could not possibly be the same as before he entered the ring, and Ali was a pitcher. Think of all the catchers, the guys who took three to give one, the crowd pleasers, the club fighters, the meat, the stiff, the tomato cans, the ham-and-eggers. Boxing is full of brain damage."

Yet Wiley also spends considerable time exploring the culture from which professional boxing emerges, including accounts of several lengthy visits with Emanuel Stewart, who taught boxing as a rehabilitation activity at a public gymnasium in Detroit and also managed and promoted certain fighters on the side. Wiley thinks it obvious that Stewart himself was doing a good job as a part of a system that is not to be smugly written off by easy idealists who would ignore the complex social pressures out of which it arises. Even so, there is no getting around it: "If you fight for twenty years, you're lucky if all you end up with is slurred consonants and a memory that blinks." The book ends, memorably and in consummate irony, with the description of an encounter with Ali, seated alone by a window in the sunlight at an airport, "in dark glasses, unbothered, looking straight ahead. Serene."

These days some of the more informative writing about boxing, and about sports in general, is being done by Gerald Early, a literature and American studies scholar. In a book of essays, *The Culture of Bruising* (1994), as well as in earlier pieces, he views the fight game as a phenomenon of a dehumanizing modern society, not as some kind of stylized artistic reenactment of mankind's primitive aggressiveness, and he characterizes the boxer as offering "a pantomime of rebellion totally devoid of any political content except ritualized male anger turned into a voyeuristic fetish." In so offering, the boxer also "symbolizes, in some respects, the individual in mass society: marginalized, alone, and consumed by the very demands and acts of his consumption. Bruising is a kind of dumb play of the human crisis of identity in the modern society." Now this is heady talk, and Early does tend to serve up generalizations like a short-order cook. Unlike all too many conceptualizing critics, however, he proceeds to develop such ideas into quite illuminating discussions.

He has much to say about the significance of the Floyd Patterson–Sonny Liston heavyweight fight of September 1962, in which Patterson, whom Early characterizes as "one of the most thoughtful men ever to enter the boxing ring," was knocked out by the burly ex-con and onetime labor goon in the first round. Patterson, in what he wrote and said, exemplifies for Early the middle-class black accommodationist liberalism of the 1950s and early 1960s, and just as that stance came to be discredited in favor of a view of black achievement that did not consist of demonstrating one's "respectability," so Liston's savage demolition of Patterson was in effect the ushering in of the militancy of the later 1960s. In Early's words, "Liston laughed at Patterson's pretension as if to say: 'What do white folks care about your dignity; if they cared at all would you even be a fighter? Face it, chump, you're a bruiser just as I am, no better and no worse.' That black cynicism blew like a harsh wind across the land, blowing through all black folks' windows and, to borrow a phrase, pushing the bad air out."

Early has a remarkable essay, "The Romance of Toughness," on the ghostwritten autobiographies of Jake LaMotta (*Raging Bull*) and Rocky Graziano (*Somebody Up There Likes Me*), two battlers of the 1940s and 1950s. These two middleweights had ugly, violent childhoods, spent time in reform schools, and did prison terms. LaMotta was one of the most disliked fighters of his day; he was involved with racketeers, threw at least one fight, and was known for the wild viciousness of his fighting style. Graziano, not as durable a battler, was even so a solid puncher who won through to respectability and, briefly, a championship. "Graziano's is the story of human reclamation; LaMotta's is the story of human waste, the absolute impossibility of achieving true human reclamation. LaMotta's moral is that we must learn to live with ourselves. Graziano's is that we can learn to be somebody else."

The author sees in these autobiographies no argument for success in the prize ring as a way of transcending the psychological wounds of a disadvantaged upbringing, as apologists for boxing would claim: "it is the sheerest nonsense to propose that the terror on the streets can be ended by selling it as a performance in a prize ring, always the self-serving argument of those of the modern world who wish to find some redeeming social worth in the sport without quite having to resort to the idea that it is the only way a poor, brutal, and brutalized kid could make a great deal of money."

There remains the question of why boxing has ceased to function as an accredited form of middle-class recreation. What drove it from the athletic programs of schools and colleges, and now restricts it to the ghettos and barrios of the inner cities where at most it can attract some few kids off the streets and into gyms, was the inescapable and flagrant fact of its brutality. The open intent was to hit a human being sufficiently hard to knock him unconscious, preferably by a blow to the head or heart. Unlike almost all other contact sports, there was no pursuit of ball or puck going on to distract the audience from contemplation of sheer violence. Not even the legalized mayhem that takes place in professional football has as its principal objective the deliberate paralyzing of one's opponent. Whatever boxing's literary and cultural charms, those participating were all too apt to end up brain-damaged or worse. The medical associations had been warning about this for years. The statistics were undeniable.

The authorities finally gave in. The high schools and colleges and, except in the blighted districts of the larger cities, the public recreation departments stopped sponsoring it. Devotees can still watch it on television here and there, but it has lost most of its social respectability. Aspiring young sports-reporters-to-be no longer convene at ringsides to chronicle heroic exploits, or dream of some day doing so in the working-press row at Soldier Field or Madison Square Garden. Were he coming along today, Ernest Hemingway would have to find another off-hour guise. Come to think of it, he *would* have looked good dressed for kung-fu.

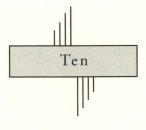

POLEMICAL CODA: OUR ABSOLUTELY DEPLORABLE LITERARY SITUATION—AND SOME THOUGHTS ON HOW TO FIX IT GOOD

I close this chronicle with a disclaimer. This is, that I am not ordinarily given to gloomy cultural prognostication, and have always suspected most such laments as being at bottom variations on the age-old motif of the Death of the Gods. I may also be a victim of creeping senectitude: *O tempora! O mores!* as Cicero put it. Yet notwithstanding that, I have to say that the American literary situation as it is shaping up nowadays is, to anyone who believes that literature is something more than diversionary reading, enough to drive a prudent observer to strong drink.

I propose to deal in practical, not theoretical, terms, focusing my resentment not on problems of spiritual malaise, cultural degeneration, the failure of the center to hold, and so on, but on such crass matters as readership, audience, and commerce in general. For if good books cannot get published because the big publishing houses are concentrating on better-paying junk, and if it is almost impossible for readers to find out about worthy new books because these seldom get reviewed, then what chance will even the most accomplished young contemporary author have to get a book before the public?

From the standpoint of getting good books published and read, the belles lettres, as we used to call them, are in dubious shape and getting worse. Poetry, as an artistic genre meant to be read by a general literary audience, is dead in the market. Literary fiction is still breathing, but the prognosis is melancholy. As for criticism—well, in the sense of having anything to do with the function of helping to sort out and make accessible what is being written by working poets and novelists, it scarcely even exists any more. It now looks, I regret to say, as if Marshall McLuhan might have been correct, and the Age of Gutenberg is rapidly on the way out, having been succeeded by the Age of the Television Set.*

What is happening is approximately as follows:

1. More money can be made in pop culture—television, middlebrow costume romance, mass market paperbacks, assorted gimmickry and self-help, and so on—than in literature.

2. Because the commercial medium whereby literature is published and sold is the same as those whereby the artifacts of popular culture are marketed, the profit-and-loss performance of literature is being evaluated by people who are chiefly in business to sell mass market cultural products. It is as if the choice of titles to be issued by the Cuala Press had been left up to the publishers of the *Guinness World Records*.

3. Literature today, in short, is more or less in the situation of a motherless adolescent whose father has remarried and whose stepmother doesn't much care for the presence of teenagers around the house.

The outcome of such a happenstance is inevitable. As noted, poetry is now a cottage industry, and literary fiction is stumbling. The television tube is in large measure responsible for this, because it has virtually obliterated the common ground that once existed between literature and pop culture. Today it is either Judith Krantz or Eudora Welty, John Jakes or John Barth. There is little or no overlap any more, for the reason that the expectations of the general audience have been tailored to the aesthetic dimensions of the TV set. Why bother to sort out and explore the emotional and intellectual subtleties of a good novel, when television can make everything so simple, clear, and direct?

Except for what can be managed through snob appeal—not an inconsiderable factor in the spread of culture, to be sure—it has become ex-

---

* As for the most recent technological innovation, the Internet, it does not seem to me that as presently constituted it is a major factor in what I have been lamenting, inasmuch as it requires reading. Anyway, let us hope.

tremely difficult to sell good literary fiction to a large audience, and apparently it isn't going to get any easier in the years to come. For, to repeat, by removing the experience of complexity in culture, television is adulterating the aesthetic taste of all but the more resolute and dedicated readers.

The result is that we are coming to have two kinds of readers—a small, mostly academic-trained audience; and a vast middlebrow commercial audience. The former is served by little magazines, literary quarterlies, university presses, and certain small publishing houses, most of them without national distribution in most bookstores. The latter, which reads no poetry or criticism and only some fiction, is serviced by the same publication outlets that sell books and magazines to the mass audience.

The middlebrow clientele can still be persuaded to buy certain literary works, if these are cleverly packaged and prominently endorsed by TV celebrities. But it is cultural sleight of hand: read this novel because Oprah Winfrey says it's good. The analogy is with encouraging people to buy chocolate-coated cookies as a way of supporting the Girl Scouts of America.

The magazines that used to span the gap between highbrow and middle—the *New Yorker, Harper's,* the *Atlantic,* and others—no longer do so. They have angled over toward the middlebrows and now strive to provide reading matter designed for use before and after watching television.

Under these circumstances, what has happened is that the literary practitioner coming onto the scene today faces the option of either retreating into the academy or else becoming a branch of show business. On the one hand there is a literature written for and read mainly by literary professionals; on the other there is fiction published and marketed according to the star system. Those authors who seem potentially exploitable as celebrities are given essentially the same kind of promotion as Hollywood figures and presidential candidates, and then judged by how well they can conduct themselves as public entertainers. A novelist who is unwilling or unable to embark on an extensive author's tour, or who can't be made to perform colorfully on a network talk show, is out of it; he or she had better go looking for a teaching position.

How, other than through use of the techniques of applied showbiz, can an author of a new book hope to get it noticed and read? By good reviews? The odds are heavily against it. Compare the book review situation now to what it was even as recently as a few decades ago. A novel coming out in the 1940s and 1950s, if it were more than usually promising, might well receive three reviews in publications with other than regional circulation—in the *New York Times Book Review,* the *Herald-Tribune Books* supplement, and the *Saturday Review.* If one of the three chose not to review the book, or if its review was uncomprehending and dismissive, the book still had two other chances at being properly noticed. Moreover, the news magazines reviewed lots of books each week; the *Atlantic* and *Harper's* were still literary publications; and both the *New Republic* and the *Nation* had strong book sections edited by literary figures of genuine stature.

Today the *Trib* and the *Saturday Review* are gone. The only newspaper of national circulation that makes a substantial effort to cover the book publishing scene is the *Times.* In point of fact it does its best; habitually it leans over backward not to be provincial or ultracommercial. But it can review only so many books per week, and its failure to review a book can totally wreck not only that book's chances but those of the author's next book as well.

There is the *New York Review of Books,* but it is utterly unconcerned with new fiction, and its provincialism can be almost beyond belief. *USA Today* devotes scarcely more serious attention to books than it does to stamp collecting; it has only a scant literary presence. The *Village Voice* is a scruffy affair designed to be read at unisex hair salons. *Harper's?* The *Atlantic?* As well look for coverage of a first novel in the *Daily Racing Form.* The *New Republic* and the *Nation?* They have long since ceased to count for anything much in the literary cosmos.

The melancholy fact is that other than getting a prominent review in the *New York Times,* which is possible but unlikely, the only way that a good novel by an unknown writer can receive any attention other than of a local or at most a regional nature is to get noticed on National Public Radio. But that is a dubious proposition, because NPR is a branch of the entertainment industry, and those in charge of selecting the books to be spotlighted are looking for "angles"—that is, controversial or off-the-beaten-track content, not literary mastery.

I have been discoursing principally in terms of the obstacles faced by unpublished fiction writers. When it comes to poets, there is no hope at all—for there is simply no such thing as a national audience reading poetry any more, nor has there been for at least a quarter century. It is a cottage industry, with the clientele mainly drawn from the immediate geographical area. No consensus exists; good poets who have published a half-dozen or more volumes cannot assume that their new work will be noticed and reviewed anywhere whatever.

Almost all the commercial book publishing houses have long since given up bringing out collections of new poems; university presses and small imprints now do the book publishing. The poets earn their livelihood by giving readings, teaching, and collecting fellowships. The few big national prizes are largely controlled by a handful of poets and hangers-on clustered mainly in and around Cambridge, Massachusetts, and Morningside Heights. But to win a Pulitzer or Bollingen Prize for verse doesn't remotely mean what it once did, anyway. No longer do readers go rushing to the bookstores in search of the prize-winning volumes when the announcements are made. If they did they might well not find them there, for the simple reason that most stores don't stock new verse any more. The practice of poetry has never been a particularly remunerative affair, but nowadays it is at close to rock bottom in public presence. It reminds me somehow of ice fishing. You have to want to go fishing awfully badly to do it at all. Fortunately, some still do.

As for criticism, which is to say writings about writing, we have the odd spectacle of an intense academic interest in literary theory, and almost none, academic or otherwise, in understanding, evaluating, and sorting out the literature being written today. Newspaper book reviews are the beginning and the end of it. The literary role that used to be played by the magazine critics—such as Mencken in the *Mercury,* Cowley in the *New Republic,* Krutch in the *Nation,* Wilson in the *New Yorker*—doesn't get played any more. Except for a few newspaper critics such as Yardley in the *Washington Post,* the idea that there could be a coherent, identifiable critical viewpoint about contemporary letters, articulated in a single place and offering consistent commentary on the literary scene, appears to be as dated as the Stutz Bearcat.

To return again to the situation of the novel, in which at least a degree of general reader interest is still maintained, consider the situation as it is confronted by a young writer without influential connections and without an established New York–based literary agent, who hopes to break into print. The day when such a person could mail off a manuscript to one of the big trade publishing houses, and if possessing talent expect to have that talent recognized and editorial guidance offered to bring it to fruition, has almost totally vanished from ken. Many of the big houses won't read unsolicited manuscripts. Even those that do keep a recent Sarah Lawrence or Fairleigh Dickinson graduate on the payroll to glance at what comes in over the transom rely primarily upon what is sent them by literary agents.

The missing element in today's book publishing, from the standpoint of the young author hoping to get a book accepted, is, simply, *editing.* This is because the economics of the industry will no longer accommodate the system whereby so many of our best American writers got their first books published and their careers launched. The kind of editor who used to take pride in identifying potential literary merit in the unsponsored manuscript of a young author, and work with that author over a period of time, often through several drafts, to bring that potential talent to published fruition, is as rare nowadays as Leopold Bloom's roc's auk's egg.

Unless a book is already close to publishable form when submitted, few editors would dare take a chance on it. To spend numerous hours reading successive drafts and writing lengthy directives for a first novel that will very likely lose money when published, whatever the future literary prospects of the author, is no way to hold on to an editorial job in trade publishing today. Nobody in a position of corporate authority is going to be impressed by the thought that, red ink notwithstanding, a potentially distinguished talent is being brought along.

To offer a young author a modest option on a book, much less an actual contract to publish, an editor must first gain the approval of an editorial committee. Given the configuration of big-time trade publishing today, the deciding vote will very likely be cast by the senior editor, who has just negotiated a contract, with a $750,000 advance, for a still-to-be-written history of the sex life of the Kennedy family, including in-laws, and is already under fire from the soap company conglomerate owning the house for having failed to turn a seven-figure profit for two publishing seasons in a row.

Do I exaggerate unduly? If you think so, examine the book trade news in successive issues of *Publishers Weekly* for a month or so. There you will see what publishing is mostly about in our time. As for the shades of Max Perkins, Hiram Haydn, Alfred Knopf, John Farrar, Ferris Greenslet, Alfred Harcourt, Ben Huebsch, Jim Henle, and all the others, if any such were brought back to life and asked to listen in on an editorial staff conclave at most of the big houses today, they would believe themselves to be not at a book publishing meeting in New York City but a marketing session on the MGM lot in Culver City, California.

Thus the function of the editor in the post-Gutenberg era. Add to this the fact that, as noted earlier, if the young novelist's book does get accepted, properly edited, and published, the chances of its receiving the kind of serious reviewing that will call it forcefully to the attention of a sizable number of readers are quite poor, particularly if the publisher can't find a prominent TV or radio personality to testify on its behalf. What we have, in sum, is about as sour an outlook for our country's literature as has existed since James Fenimore Cooper first began publishing fiction in the early 1820s.

What then, as Lenin once remarked under somewhat different circumstances, is to be done?

Aged and overweight though I am, I have a few ideas to put forth. A decent respect to the opinions of Mankind, however, requires that they be accompanied by a declaration of the assumptions under which they have been formulated. To wit.

I believe that a decent-sized audience for good literature—call it elitist if you will—does indeed exist, and that potentially it is considerably larger than the mostly academic audience that currently supports the quarterly reviews and little magazines. Nor is it identical with the audience for avant-garde literature, though the latter can compose part of it. The distinguishing characteristic of this elite audience is that it *prefers* reading books to watching TV. As a book-buying clientele it is probably sizable enough, and affluent enough, to support the national letters, without the help of the mass entertainment industry, and without retreat into the academy.

Very well. Given those hypotheses, what needs to be done?

1. First of all, the audience for good literature must be approached as a decisive entity in itself, not as the intellectual or literary fringe of the mass middlebrow audience. In order for this to happen, it must be identified, singled out, and carefully cultivated.

2. Literature, if it is to survive and flourish, cannot continue to be oper-ated as a subsidiary branch of the cookbook and 900-telephone-number industry. The publication and dissemination of good literature must be *separated,* physically, geographically, culturally, financially, from the publi-cation and dissemination of items of interest to devotees of mass TV culture.

3. We have got to establish, or reestablish, a *literary situation* that is not part of and not dependent upon the spare venture capital of the purvey-ors of cultural pablum.

4. To do that, there must be a revival of intelligent criticism of con-temporary literature, and literary journalism about it, so as to provide focus and cohesion.

5. The key to the whole situation is the establishment of several first-class nationally distributed magazines—not literary magazines, mind you, but general-circulation magazines designed for an educated, intelligent, sophis-ticated audience, which as part of their operation would regularly review and criticize a range of new books (including new poetry).

6. In order to bring all this off, that is, to rejuvenate the national letters, a full-fledged conspiracy is needed. Those who believe that the American literary imagination is worth preserving must be encouraged to go about doing so with the same kind of proselytizing zeal with which other con-spiratorial groups such as the National Rifle Association, the Church of Jesus Christ of Latter-Day Saints, the Republican Party, and the Ameri-can Kennel Club approach the influencing of public opinion.

Is any of the above likely to happen? I give it about the same chance as the Chevrolet Division of General Motors producing an American-manufactured automobile that will merit and receive a "better-than-average" frequency-of-repair rating in the *Consumer Reports Buying Guide.* Which is to say, next to none at all. It is not only improbable; it is wildly vision-ary. Set next to it, *transition's* famed "Revolution of the Word" of the 1920s seems eminently practical.

Yet if our letters are to flourish, such a procedure, or something like it, will have to be done. The key to it, as noted earlier, is probably Item No. 5, above. What this country's literature badly needs is several well-edited periodicals, none of them either edited in or funded through New York

City, published on a monthly basis or more frequently, and offering articles, familiar essays, stories, poems, etc., directed at a "highbrow," but *not*
merely academic or avant-garde, audience. By this I decidedly do not
mean literary magazines as such; nor do I have in mind what quarterly
reviews do. These periodicals would range the spectrum of civilized curiosity, but do so for an intelligent, sophisticated audience that enjoys reading
about topics other than lawn care, antiques, and the domestic arrangements of film stars. The objective would be to produce the kind of magazine journalism that persons who like to read would read for pleasure.

Where now is the magazine that regularly provides interesting, well-
written fare for an educated and sophisticated general audience? Or put it
this way: other than in specialized publications, how many good magazine articles have *you* read recently? Would you subscribe to a periodical
of a nonscholarly, nonprofessional nature that offered a regular array of
pieces about various topics, pieces that neither insulted your intelligence
nor strove constantly to be modish and trendy? (This last is one reason
the magazines I propose must be edited outside the corporate limits of
the Big Apple.) And as part of such a periodical, wouldn't you welcome
sensible and insightful commentary about new books, written not for
academic specialists alone but for intelligent, educated readers?

Think what the existence of a few such magazines would do for our
culture. Regularly published and imaginatively edited, they would develop
and maintain a solid and devoted audience of intelligent readers, which,
though not large by mass media standards, would be quite numerous
enough—and consequential enough—to provide a foundation for a lively
literary and cultural situation. Our writers would be able to get their
books intelligently reviewed, in publications that were important enough
and widely enough circulated so that favorable critical appraisal would
carry real meaning at bookstores.

In saying that our literature must separate itself from the book and
magazine industry of the metropolitan Northeast, what I mean is that it
has got to be able to function on terms that do not require it to compete
with the commercial mass market expectations of the entertainment
industry, centered as the latter are on the television audience. The only

way to arrange that is to operate independently of it. And that cannot be done as things now stand, because the two industries, publishing and showbiz-TV, are too massively and intricately tied together up and down the line.

To state the proposition in book-business terms, obviously considerably more money is to be made from promoting a book so that it will sell 100,000 copies instead of 25,000, than from promoting a book so that it will sell 10,000 copies instead of 5,000. No publishing house, especially if owned by a conglomerate, is going to try to do both. That is why the deck is now so cruelly stacked against literary publishing. What the future welfare of our literature depends upon is the kind of book publishing that will *concentrate* on doing the latter rather than the former.

It comes down, then, simply to this: so-called print culture must be removed from the auspices of the TV-centered mass entertainment industry. It is too valuable to be allowed to go by default—which is what seems to be happening now. We are letting it dwindle away toward oblivion. It does not follow, either logically or practically, that because many more people regularly watch Geraldo than read Annie Dillard or Mark Helprin, literature is therefore doomed. But when we allow the same industry to preside over the promulgation, distribution, and critical evaluation of all three, as if they were equally engaged in showbiz, how much chance do the latter two have?

We have therefore got to sever the financial bands that have connected contemporary letters with the popular entertainment industry and let literature flourish on its own, as the product of literary folk writing for a literary audience.

We come now to the question of how it is to be done, and who is to pick up the tab for doing it. There you have me, for I haven't the slightest idea. Having identified the cat and explained why and how it is to be belled, I leave the belling to others more resourceful than myself.

I will say this, however. What the enterprise probably needs is a Sugar Daddy, someone with lots and lots of dough, addicted psychologically to swimming against the current, and known to take delight in upsetting established applecarts (I deliberately employ four clashing metaphors in a single sentence to emphasize the unreason involved). The S.D. needn't be himself a reader of the kind of literature we are out to save. It is more important that he enjoy getting involved in conspiracies for their own sake, and that he not own any substantial amount of Time-Warner stock himself. For starters, does anyone in the audience know Bill Gates?

INDEX